PUSHKIN PRESS

ENCOUNTERS
AND
DESTINIES

'At a time of monetary crisis and political disorder, of mounting border controls and barbed-wire fences... Zweig's celebration of the brotherhood of peoples reminds us that there is another way'   *The Nation*

'Zweig's accumulated historical and cultural studies... remain a body of achievement almost too impressive to take in'   Clive James

'Stefan Zweig's time of oblivion is over for good... it's good to have him back'

Salman Rushdie, *The New York Times*

'Zweig is the most adult of writers; civilised, urbane, but never jaded or cynical; a realist who nonetheless believed in the possibility—the necessity—of empathy'

Independent

'Zweig deserves to be famous again, and for good'

Times Literary Supplement

T0286644

STEFAN ZWEIG was born in 1881 in Vienna, a member of a wealthy Austrian-Jewish family. He studied in Berlin and Vienna and was first known as a translator and later as a biographer. Zweig travelled widely, living in Salzburg between the wars and enjoying literary fame. His stories and novellas were collected in 1934. In the same year, with the rise of Nazism, he briefly moved to London, taking British citizenship. After a short period in New York, he settled in Brazil. It was here that he completed his acclaimed memoir *The World of Yesterday*, a lament for the golden age of a Europe destroyed by two world wars. On 23 February 1942, Zweig and his second wife Lotte were found dead, following an apparent double suicide. Much of his work is available from Pushkin Press.

Stefan Zweig
ENCOUNTERS
AND
DESTINIES
A Farewell to Europe

Edited, Translated and with an
Introduction by Will Stone

PUSHKIN
PRESS

Pushkin Press
71–75 Shelton Street
London, WC2H 9JQ

First published by Pushkin Press in 2020

1 3 5 7 9 8 6 4 2

ISBN 13: 978-1-78227-346-2

Designed and typeset by Tetragon, London
Printed and bound by CPI Group (UK) Ltd, Croydon, CRO 4YY

www.pushkinpress.com

CONTENTS

'Art is an eternal war, never an end, always a relentless beginning'

ZWEIG ON TOSCANINI

INTRODUCTION

I

How can it be, one might be tempted to ask, that none of Stefan Zweig's corpus of elegant eulogies, elegies and tributes to his fellow artists, musicians and writers has ever appeared in the English language until now? After all, a volume entitled *Souvenirs et Rencontres*, which contained a number of those texts you are about to encounter here, appeared in France as early as 1951, only nine years after Zweig's suicide in Brazil. We, however, in time-honoured fashion, have lagged behind. Despite the recent 'Zweig renaissance' in the Anglophone world, there still remain a vast number of texts which currently lie beyond the reach of readers, glittering like an inviting estuary that imperceptibly meets the wider ocean of European literature. Here are some of them, a rich selection of those that concern the author's powerful memories of fellow travellers across European culture in the twentieth century—some, but by no means all, for Zweig relentlessly penned tributes both to his contemporaries and to those he considered great masters of the past, or artists who had represented something personally significant for him in his evolution as a writer. I have selected from this wider body of work texts which to me seemed most intriguing, engaging and vital, or which might harbour some

9

prescience of our own time. I have also chosen a range of figures across the arts which includes those who were famous at Zweig's time of writing and still are today, and others to whom our epoch has shown less generosity of spirit, either for sound reasons or no clear reason at all. One of these is the Belgian poet Emile Verhaeren. The substantial and eloquently crafted memorial which Zweig dedicates to him I have included partly because it is considered as one of Zweig's most successful pieces of biographical writing, and although admiring of his subject, eschews the hagiographic style of his earlier biography of Verhaeren (1910). It is important for readers to understand the central role Verhaeren played in Zweig's early European trajectory, and the friendship which was maintained until the rupture of war in 1914 and the Belgian's untimely death in Rouen two years later.

Zweig's book-length biographies are well known if not widely read today, partly due to the lack of modern translations and some of the older ones being out of print. Rather frustratingly, these are the most relevant for our own time. I think of *Erasmus of Rotterdam* from 1934, and *The Right to Heresy: Castellio against Calvin* from 1936, back-to-back power plays between tyrannical figures or the state and freedom-loving individuals, with Luther and Calvin standing in for Hitler and Erasmus and Castellio for Zweig. These were symbolic warnings from history superimposed on the totalitarian present. But this compulsion for literary biographies had begun much earlier with a series of monographs. In 1905, Zweig had published an important essay on the French poet Verlaine and in 1910 his major biography of Verhaeren appeared in Germany, soon being translated into French and English. The pre-war 'golden age' of 1900–14 was the time of Verhaeren's greatest influence; he was one of the most visible and sought-after European poets, filling auditoriums across the continent as far as Moscow. In addition to the biography, Zweig flung all his energies into establishing the Belgian's reputation as a major poet in Germany, translating, albeit rather freely, certain works himself, and even attempted to corral a coterie of disciples which included Rilke to translate into German between them a multi-volume *Collected Poems* of Verhaeren; but this crowning moment for the Belgian poet and high priest of the pan-Europeans was abandoned due to the outbreak of hostilities in 1914. The impulsion to ardently support and promote those writers Zweig particularly valued, to render biographical portraits as confirmations of his admiration, continued till the end of his life.

For example, in Brazilian exile, mired in morbid depression over the perceived annihilation of Europe, he by chance rediscovered Montaigne, seizing on him as his last guiding master, and set out to write the necessary tribute. Shorn of his European friends, desperate for a supportive and sympathetic voice from history, Zweig found in the lonely vigil, the apartness of Montaigne something he needed, both a fraternal counsel and an exemplary advocate of free thought. It seems that whenever Zweig was touched at the deepest point by another writer or artist, their life story or creative example, he felt an overwhelming urge to explore them further through such portraits, to flesh out the elements of his veneration. This is why, when exiled in London during the 1930s, he was often installed in the British Museum library gathering material for the works on Marie Antoinette, Magellan or Mary Queen of Scots. The public or private library was essentially Zweig's club; he had to be surrounded by books, have access to books, and whenever he was about to embark on a project he would ask his wife, Friderike von Winternitz, to order a whole list of secondary literature on his subject. A poignant photograph of Zweig taken in the summer of 1940 shows him descending the empty steps of the New York Public Library. As is well known, Zweig was an astute collector of rare books and manuscripts, some of which were lost in the traumatic years of journeying, but a significant portion of which survived and, fittingly, are now safeguarded in a library, the British Library in London. Beyond the book-length biographies, Zweig also wrote countless portraits of writers outside his own time, some almost expected and others intriguing: Goethe, Chateaubriand, Rimbaud, Dante, Jaurès, Baudelaire, Sainte-Beuve…

After the trauma of the 1914–18 war had faded, Zweig's literary output was beyond prolific. From 1919 to 1934 he based himself in an initially unheated yet palatial villa atop the Kapuzinerberg in Salzburg known as Paschinger Schlössl, but later known as Villa Europa. Here, for fifteen largely stable, trouble-free years, the great and the good of European letters ascended the steep, winding lane of the hill to the gate of No. 5. Though ever on the move, zigzagging the continent, taking advantage of the ever-denser web of Europe's railways and making regular trips to Paris, Zurich, Brussels, Rome, Berlin and Vienna, Zweig now had an anchorage, a central base, the well-oiled hub of a many-spoked wheel, not to mention a generously assisting partner who proved highly effective in promotional and organizational terms. Zweig's literary production went up a gear. In these years he wrote the portrait of Marcel Proust's bedridden resistance and Frans Masereel's Expressionist craftsmanship, issued fulsome gratitude to Romain Rolland and erected his lyrically decorous memorial to Rilke found here, but he was also busy publishing his finest short stories and novellas. During the 1920s Zweig treated his readers to a procession of great miniatures including *Compulsion* (1920), *Amok* and *Fantastic Night* (1922), *Fear* (1925), *Confusion* (1927), *The Invisible Collection* (1927) and *Mendel the Bibliophile* (1929). But alongside all this he still managed to produce his ambitious series of trilogies on world writers, *Master Builders: An Attempt at a Typology of the Spirit*. The first, *Three Masters: Balzac, Dickens, Dostoyevsky*, appeared in 1920. This was followed by *The Struggle with the Daemon: Hölderlin, Kleist, Nietzsche* (1925), and finally *Adepts in Self-Portraiture: Casanova, Stendhal, Tolstoy* (1928).

Zweig possessed an indefatigable ideal of a progressing creative humanity that was incrementally elevating consciousness for the greater good of mankind, despite twists in the road in the form of episodic acts of barbarism, war and imperial conquest. This vast historical network of artists, writers, poets, musicians and philosophers Zweig viewed as a literary and artistic family, an interlocking fraternity all working towards the same end, whose individual talent fed into the universality of cultural enlightenment, with each generation handing on a baton they had been privileged to receive from their illustrious forebears. This romantic premise forms the bedrock beneath all Zweig's works, but comes through most visibly in the historical biographies, essays on the importance of European unity, the enigmas of artistic creativity and here, in these personal tributes to his contemporaries. The reader will soon note that the language in these pieces, culled from different periods of his life, bears a simultaneous message and that there is a noticeable repetition and reinforcement, both within one piece and across others. Zweig's central tenet remains constant, like an electrical current that cannot be diverted or switched off. Always he returns to the same countenancing of his ideals of universalism, of the responsibility, the necessity of actively tending culture, hard won over a millennia, and not only of admiring it but—crucially—reseeding it. Faced with external threats, with indifference or hostility, this demands an individual act of heroism, but for Zweig not in an isolated, inspired act, in a moment of fiery convulsion, but through a kind of drawn-out inspirational labour, where commitment and patience carry as much weight as the visionary element.

It is important to note that in these fifteen pieces, the western half of Europe is widely represented through the nationalities of those discussed: France, Switzerland, Germany, Belgium, Austria, England, Ireland. Zweig's wide-ranging travels in 'his' Europe and some exotic forays beyond meant the conveyance of ever-greater numbers of writers and artists to his terrace above Salzburg, and when he did not meet them personally, he warmly and enthusiastically received their books and correspondence. Here was a financially secure man of letters purposely based at the heart of the continent, keenly surveying the literary and artistic landscape from his eyrie for initiatives of note which might serve to enrich his life experience, or that pertained to his own work. Then, either by mail, a personal visit or train journey, that creative spirit, that rare manuscript, that fateful book would be absorbed into the whole. But by 1933–34 it was all over: as Hitler in triumph descended from the Obersalzberg some thirty kilometres distant to begin his drive for European subjugation, Zweig descended the Kapuzinerberg to relinquish the privileged life of a man of letters and begin that of a Jewish refugee, abandoning Salzburg for exile in London.

II

A number of the pieces here were destined to be read at events, such as the funerals of Freud and Roth, at a memorial for Rilke, a ceremonial occasion for Hofmannsthal, a special birthday celebration for Schnitzler and Gorky. Most of those figures represented here were men Zweig knew personally, even intimately, yet the tone of his texts can appear quite different. Compare, for example, the more formal, reverential style of those to Romain Rolland and Rilke, both of whom Zweig had known for long years across the abyss of war and admired profoundly for different reasons, and the less ornate and earnest personal reminiscence of, rather than elegy to, the English writer John Drinkwater, with whom Zweig was less familiar. The Drinkwater text was written midway through Zweig's London exile, ten years later than the other two, and feels noticeably more modern to our eyes. There is the humanity here of an observer, a newcomer, rather than one penning a devotional eulogy. There is something moving and strangely timeless about this Drinkwater curiosity, with its window into the world of writers and intellectuals in the London of the time, assembling for a private viewing of Drinkwater's coronation film. But although there is a difference in coloration to all these portraits, a certain darkness is manifest in them all, in spite of Zweig's strenuous efforts to bring to the fore his subjects' creative achievements, their stoicism and heroism.

This presence of death suffuses Zweig's works, whether fiction or non-fiction; the spectre of suicide often makes its entrance, and it was Montaigne's essay 'A Custom of the Isle of Cea' which provided a catalytic historical affirmation or example for Zweig's decision to exit the world by his own hand.

But death and its challenging reality of severance is not the only story Zweig is telling in his paean to Freud beside the casket in Golders Green Cemetery, likewise with Roth; but it is what lurks in all the texts as the mortal turning point when the immortal spirit of the work, not the living man, is released from the finite physical debris. In 'Marcel Proust's Tragic Life Course', Zweig issues a rallying cry in the death chamber of a bedridden Proust, swaddled in cravats, who overcomes the fear of death by listening to it so attentively. From the opening line, when we picture the struggling writer seeking to subsist long enough to get down the material which is backing up in his head and heart, everything is moving one way; and although in its passage downstream the log may catch on the bank from time to time, eventually the irresistible flow takes it over the lip of the falls. Likewise, 'The Return of Gustav Mahler' is dominated by the moving moment when Zweig, aboard a transatlantic liner which also bears the dying Mahler below decks, finally lays eyes on his hero in the 'remorqueur' (tugboat) which carries them to the dockside:

> I finally saw him: he lay there, pale as one already in the grip of death, inanimate, with closed lids. The breeze had swept his greying hair to one side, his arched brow projected clearly and boldly, and below was that firm chin, where the power of his will sat. The withered hands lay folded on the blanket, for the first time I really saw him, the fiery one, enfeebled. But this silhouette, unforgettable, unforgettable! was set against a grey infinitude of sky and sea, immeasurable grief was in this gaze but also something transfigured by greatness, something that

faded into the sublime, like music. I knew then that I
had witnessed him for the last time.

Then there is the affecting 'Mater Dolorosa'. Zweig had already
written an inspired portrait of Nietzsche drawn from the
period of the philosopher's wanderings in the Engadine and
latterly in Turin in *The Struggle with the Daemon: Hölderlin, Kleist,
Nietzsche* in 1925. Here Zweig pinpointed Nietzsche's malaise, his
gradually ebbing strength and desperate fate, artfully portraying the hushed exits and entrances of the solitary, the myopic
'Professor', socially adrift in the austere dining rooms of Alpine
pensions and boarding houses. 'Mater Dolorosa' stands as an
addendum to the earlier text, but focuses on the heroism of
Nietzsche's mother, who, though locked in her provinciality and
deeply ashamed of her troubled son's blasphemy, nevertheless
devoted what remained of her life to caring for the stricken
philosopher–leviathan. One feels here that Zweig's sympathy
for his subject is authentic:

> The unintentional gesture proves always the most beauti-
> ful and the most human. The purest emotions always
> issue from the simple, from the unadorned and factual
> truth and therefore we know more from these records of
> a simple woman than from all the clinical evidence and
> scholarly dissertations around the downfall and death
> of this mighty spirit of the past generation.

'Arturo Toscanini: A Life Portrait' presents the legendary
composer as the single-minded battler for elusive perfection,
the loner and derided obsessive ploughing on in the face of
a hurricane of criticism, suspicion and misunderstanding,

desperately trying to meld his new personal vision with the greater unifying forces of art, where it will be accepted if only the contemporary doubters don't sink the knife in. Zweig's Toscanini, like Zweig's Mahler, is a visionary wildly out of his time, shipwrecked on an island called earth in the first decades of the twentieth century where few of the native creatures understand what he is creating. Toscanini is a man with a divine mission, whose fury and crazed gestures of frustration in the rehearsal room are almost lost on the orchestra and those who have not yet caught up with his vision racing ahead of the present. This makes for a dramatic spectacle where Zweig can summon all his own imaginative forces to unleash a firestorm of imagery to communicate the mysterious, overarching tension and straining will that accompany the creative act and whose progeny is the longed-for perfected work. But that perfection, as Zweig is at pains to state here and in the Rilke piece, is off-limits to mankind and is the sole property of the gods. Yet this does not matter, because Toscanini will nevertheless hammer away, and through sheer commitment to his cause will reach by sheer force of will, if not perfection, a higher realm.

As already indicated, Zweig enjoyed long-standing close friendships with around two-thirds of those represented here, the exceptions being Mahler, Nietzsche, Proust, Gorky and Hofmannsthal. Zweig's long friendship with the Belgian wood-cut master Frans Masereel is little known, yet Zweig vaunted Masereel's art, as well as that of another Belgian artist, Léon Spilliaert, from the moment he was introduced to them through Verhaeren. He made generous purchases of their work as an enthusiast rather than a dealer, and formed lasting friendships. Zweig's eloquent overview of Masereel's woodcuts feels penetrating and must have been groundbreaking. Zweig extols his friend's modernity—'Masereel is as refreshing as anything in the natural world'—and makes a case for the Belgian artist's unflinching scenes of modern city life as being something genuinely new in art, and his method of production as bearing a direct link to the patient labour and eye for detail of the old masters of German art. But above all Zweig argues that, like Rubens, Tolstoy, Whitman and Balzac, Masereel is an organically unifying force, one who strives for truth in his own time so as to join a common truth for all time, a spiritual universality to which he is adding his individual effort; and he achieves this through dogged labour and the stringent acceptance of all realities, by recording every detail as he passes:

> In his wordless picture-novels *25 Images of a Man's Passion*, *The Idea* and *The Sun*, in his imaginary autobiography, he laid bare all the drives and impulses around the freedom of the individual faced with hostile powers, employing grotesque caricatures he paraded the warmongers, speculators, judges, police, all the representatives of a selfish morality, a selfish motive. His idea of the world tolerates nothing that violates the world, any single group that stymies the sacred unity of the universe. His genius is always targeted at the whole: like Whitman, who seeks to distil the world into a thousand stanzas, he wants to distil the world into images, to portray them in boundless complexity through thousands of details, without ever compromising that sense of unity.

The Zweig–Roth friendship, with its shadowy elements of interdependence, has been pored over and confused by sometimes unhelpful subjective interpretations. However, if Zweig's genuine love of Roth as a man and as a writer could ever have been in doubt, then this eulogy must surely silence any such aspersions. The tribute to Roth is one of the most complete and rewarding graveside encomiums, for one can vividly sense the personal emotion, the genuine sorrow at losing such a beloved companion of the road, an exceptional writer, whom Zweig was the first to admit wielded literary powers that outstripped his own, in such deplorable circumstances. Zweig acquits himself tactfully yet truthfully through the grim terrain, expressing the haunting reality of Roth's decline and the futility of being a spectator, the horror of looking on as a loved one pursues a path of self-destruction: 'Unbearable to watch a friend's heart murder the rest of his being and not be able to haul him to safety.'

Zweig paints a plausible picture of Roth's background and complex make-up—the Jewish man, the Russian man and the Austrian man—and how these elements interacted even in their antagonism to each other to produce a writer of genius. He reconstructs the fateful apparatus of Roth's existence, the succession of cruel life blows he received, culminating with his wife Friederike vanishing into the sanatorium stricken with schizophrenia, and Hitler's arrival in the Chancellery in 1933. Once again Zweig reaches for the familiar motif of the solitary misjudged perfectionist, toiling against the mediocrity around him. Like Nietzsche bent low over his manuscript in his pension room, Roth scribbles into his notebook at his table in Austrian coffee house, Amsterdam bar, Ostend hotel terrace or Parisian café:

> I would often run into him scribbling away at his beloved coffee-house table and knew that the manuscript had been sold in advance: he needed money, the publishers

were pressing him. But pitilessly, the most severe and sagacious judge, he ripped the pages apart before my eyes and began all over again, just because some minor epithet did not seem to have the right weight, a sentence did not exude the fullest musical sound. Faithful to his genius as to himself, he has gloriously exalted himself in his art and risen out of his own death.

Finally, there are three men here who were not only close friends at particular points of Zweig's life but older masters to observe, listen to and learn from, for Zweig was always in need of such models. The first was Verhaeren and the last Freud. In the middle was Rolland, who takes up the greatest number of years. Only Freud appears to have a bearing on the intellectual climate today, for Verhaeren fell out of favour with the reading public soon after his death: in a post-war world his ardent pantheistic verses praising human endeavour in a technological age did not appear relevant to a devastated European society struggling to explain the industrial slaughter of its young men. However, Verhaeren's earlier poetry, a unique melding of morbid symbolism and fiery evocations of nature, found favour with German Expressionist writers and even Russian Futurists. In a similar way, Rolland, author of the then widely read *Jean-Christophe* series of novels, and the controversial 'Above the Mêlée' pacifist of 1914, was later compromised for Zweig by his ill-starred flirtations with communism and fell into relative obscurity after the next world conflagration.

Verhaeren's influence on Zweig's early years cannot be underestimated, and the importance that this shepherd of transnationalism (popularly perceived as a 'European Walt Whitman') held for Zweig is encapsulated in the 'Memories of Emile Verhaeren', which he wrote seven years after the biography, in the year following Verhaeren's unexpected death. For the war had intervened, Verhaeren was now gone and the two friends had been unable to restore their friendship throughout 1914–16, due to the sealing of borders and breakdown in communication. In 1914 Verhaeren, contrary to his whole moral ethos, learnt of the invading Germany army's depraved massacres of 6,500 Belgian civilians and the burning to the ground of the priceless ancient library of Louvain. The most widely read foreign poet in Germany in 1913 was reeling in shock, his internationalist dreams shattered. This malaise culminated in his book *La Belgique sanglante* ('Belgium Bleeding') published in 1915, a vicious and lurid nationalistic harangue against German culture. His great friend and supporter Zweig was suddenly persona non grata, though the more hermetic Rilke was spared. But in the months leading up to his death Verhaeren appeared to have mellowed, having been counselled by friends on Zweig's behalf. At the eleventh hour he realized his bellicose rhetoric for what it was, his guard was lowered, the bitterness gave way, it seemed the two men were poised for a reconciliation. It was this pain of what might have been and the two years lost before Verhaeren's fatal accident in Rouen in November 1916 which propelled Zweig to write his memorial text. Zweig wished painstakingly to articulate what Verhaeren's presence had meant to his development as a writer, from the moment he chased him down like a hunter his quarry, meeting him in the summer of 1902 at the house of the sculptor Van der Stappen, where Verhaeren was sitting for a bust, until the moment in August 1914 when he was forced to break off his annual visit to Verhaeren's cottage in the Borinage and hurry back to Vienna from Ostend on one of the last trains out before the border closed. A passage in *The World of Yesterday* (1941) was evidently sourced from these 'Memories'. The following excerpt encapsulates the qualities of Verhaeren which so impressed the young, untested Zweig, keen to wrest himself from the suffocating and precocious literary atmosphere of Vienna. Zweig was seeking a less constrained world beyond, and Belgium, with its influx of cultures, felt like it lived up to its name as 'the crossroads of Europe'—he was inexorably drawn there. But once more Belgium was also to be a crossroads for warring enemies and the scene of some of the first episodes of modern barbarism in Europe:

> He always returned home from every place and every thing enriched by random experience, and this enthusiasm had become a divine custom… With the first word, he reached right into the person, for he himself was open and accessible to every new thing, never negative, always prepared to embrace all. He launched himself with his entire being, so to speak, out beyond himself, and hundreds of times I have seen this overwhelming, stormy impact of his being on others. Of me he still knew nothing, yet he was already filled with gratitude for my sake, he already took me into his confidence simply because he had learnt that I had some connection to his work. And spontaneously, before that powerful impact of his being, all sense of shyness left me. I felt free as never before in the presence of this curious, open man. His gaze, strong, steely and clear, unlocked the heart.

It is the 26th of September 1939, twenty-two years later and the opening month of a new world war in a Europe which appears radically different. Zweig, an exile in London uncertain of his future, has been invited to read the eulogy at the memorial service for his friend Sigmund Freud. What is interesting in this address is that although Zweig liberally praises Freud's achievements in intellectual terms and confirms his immortality through his works, it is the repeated insistence of his moral compass, his concern for humanity which shines through. In the end it is the humanistic element, freedom of thought and the sanctity of the creative impulse, that interests Zweig and is reiterated here. Zweig slips back to his childhood in Vienna to the moment when this craving began:

> We all dreamt, as boys, of meeting such a spiritual hero on whom we could model ourselves and whom we could aspire to, a man indifferent to the temptations of fame and vanity, a man with a full and responsible soul purely devoted to his task, a task which in turn serves not itself but the whole of humanity. This impassioned dream of our boyhood, this even more severe postulate of our mature years, was filled by this dead man's life in an unforgettable way, granting us an unprecedented spiritual contentment.

In this single excerpt Zweig reveals the ambition for his own self, the discipline required for greatness: to draw from the source of inwardness and exploit the gift in a creatively defined way, to connect with the universal spirit, to relinquish the *vanitas* of fame, to show responsibility to something greater than oneself, in the service of art, not divisive nationalist utopias, to dedicate oneself to patient labour in order to achieve such a task. If we turn to the book on Erasmus, defending his impartiality, or the free thinker Castellio, courageously resisting alone the mono-maniacal Calvin, if we look again and again at Zweig's charac-ters and subjects, the same message is present: the solitary artist somehow forcing his vision through the clay of his too slowly registering time, carving out a narrow space in history even through personal sacrifice, to overcome the always re-forming reactionary forces which seek the imagination's confinement.

WILL STONE
Exmoor, 2020

THE RETURN OF
GUSTAV MAHLER

(1915)

H E HAS COME HOME, the great exile of the past, returned in glory to the city that he, as an outcast, departed only a few years ago. In the same hall where formerly his compelling will exercised its demonic effect, his long-absent nature now takes on new spiritual form, resounding in the work. Nothing can restrain it, not opprobrium or rancour; irresistibly burgeoning with its unique qualities, feeling the purer for no longer being locked in struggle, it now fills and expands our inner world. No war, no event could hinder this elemental blossoming of his fame, and the same man who appeared to people here as something of an irritant and almost a monster has overnight become consoler and liberator. Pain and loss— his *Kindertotenlieder* express his spirit more powerfully than any others of the time, and who today does not wish to learn, with empathy, how sorrow transmogrifies itself through depth of feeling in his farewell song, the 'Song of the Earth'? Never was Gustav Mahler so revitalized and inspired by this city as now, when he is far removed from us and the ungrateful city that abandoned him is his eternal homeland. Those who truly loved him were patiently awaiting this hour, but now that it has come it scarcely brings us joy. For while he was engaged in work, our desire was to witness his creations, see them come alive. And now that they have achieved renown, it is he himself we long for, the man who will not return.

Because for us, an entire generation, he was far more than a musician, a master, a conductor, more than an artist: he was the unforgettable presence of our youth. To be young ultimately means to be conscious of the extraordinary, of some wondrously beautiful happening that transcends the narrow world of appearances, of a phenomenon, the fulfilment of a once-dreamt vision. And everything, admiration, enthusiasm, humility—they all stir up powers of devotion, of exuberance, they only seem so fiery and chaotic when concentrated in unfinished beings, burning deep within when they appear—recognized as such or intimated—in art, in love. And there is a certain grace in experiencing such fulfilment in art, in those days of premature, unspent love to observe something truly meaningful, yet free with the fullest flow of feeling. It happened to us. Anyone who has experienced those ten years of opera from Mahler's youth has enriched his life in ways that cannot be measured in words. With the keen sense of impatience, we sensed from the outset the rare thing, the miracle he harboured, the demonic man, the rarest of all, one who isn't entirely at one with creativity, but with something far more mysterious in its essence, possessing a distinctly natural power, the inspired element. There is nothing to distinguish it from the external, the influence it exerts constitutes its own singularity, something indescribable, which can only be compared to a certain magical arbitrariness of nature. It can be likened to the magnet; thousands of iron filings may cling to it. All are tragic. They know only how to plunge downwards, commanded by their inner weight, alien to all else and inactive. But there is one piece of iron, seemingly no brighter or richer than any of the rest, which inwardly retains a power, the power of stars or the furthest depths of the earth, that pulls all relatives together, weaves its own form and frees itself from the internal weight. What the magnet seizes it enlivens through its own power; if it can hold it long enough, its secret flows forth. It draws towards it kindred metals in order to enter them, dividing itself without weakening the whole: its very nature and instinct are effect. And this power—whether from the stars or the remotest depths of the earth—constitutes the will of the demonic man. Thousands mill around him, thousand upon thousand, each one rushing headlong into his own life, inherently tragic and inanimate. But he drags them towards himself, he fills the essence of the oblivious with his own will, his rhythm; he propagates himself in them by animating them. Through a kind of hypnosis, he forces them all to draw near, tensing their nerves in time with his own, wrenching them often painfully into his rhythm. He enslaves them, imposes his will on them, lends the willing something of the mystery of his force. It is precisely this demonic will that was in Mahler, a power which suppressed and resisted all opposition, but also one that inspired and enriched. About him was a molten sphere where everyone seemed to glow, always fiery, but working towards clarity. It was impossible to resist. They say that sometimes musicians tried, but his will was just too hot: all resistance simply melted. With unrivalled energy he transforms his entire world of singers, assistants, directors, musicians, moulding the chaotic interplay of hundreds of individuals into his single unit in the space of a mere three hours. He literally wrenches the will from them, he hammers, pounds and files their individual qualities, he drives them on, already they are aglow with fervour, moving inexorably into his rhythm, until the point when he has salvaged the unique from the ordinary, art from enterprise, until he is fulfilled in the work and the work is fulfilled in him.

And, magically, all flows from the external to him, all he needs he seems to find, but it finds him. Female singers are needed, rich, fiery natures, in order to bring Wagner and Mozart into being: summoned by him (or rather, unconsciously willed by the demon within) arise Mildenburg and Gutheil; a painter in order to provide an animated backdrop to the animated music, and he discovers Alfred Roller. Whatever he shares a connection with, whatever he needs to make the work complete appears suddenly as if by magic, and the stronger the personalities involved, the more passionate becomes his own. Everything is mysteriously drawn to him, slips submissively into his will, and on such evenings a work, a crowd, a house suddenly forms around him, as if for him alone. Out of his baton pulses the rhythm of our blood: just as a lightning rod binds together the tension of the whole atmosphere, so it binds the sum of our pent-up feeling. Never before in the performing arts have I experienced such unity as on these countless evenings, a unity where the purity of effect can only be aligned with the elemental, a landscape with sky, clouds and the breath of the season, that inadvertent harmonious unity of things which become present only for oneself, undiscriminating and impartial. In those days we young people learnt to love the art of perfection in him, through his example we came to understand that amidst our fragmented world it is still possible for the heightened, demonic will to construct – for an hour, two hours – the eternal, the flawless, out of fragile earthly material. In those days he became both educator and guide. No one then wielded commensurable power over us.

And so powerful was this demonic genius of his inner self that it burst through the thin layer of his outer being like a jet of flame, for he was always burning up, barely able to suppress the heat beneath the delicate crust of his corporeality. Observing him just once, you had the feeling you knew his soul. Everything about him was in a state of tension, brimming over, saturated with passion, something flickered about him like the sparks around a Leyden jar. Fury was his natural element, the only capable force, at rest he seemed pent up, when he was sat still it was as if electricity still crackled over him. It was impossible to imagine him idle, sauntering along or in gentle mood of reverie, the overheated state of his inner cauldron always demanded more power to drive on, push forward, to be perennially active. He was always en route to a destination, as if borne on a great storm, and all else seemed too leaden for him; maybe he just felt an innate aversion to real life because it was brittle, crude, shiftless, because it was all earth, weight and resistance and he sought access to the other that lay behind things, at the very furthest point of art, where this world reaches into the celestial vault. He yearned to find a path through, past these intermediate forms and on to the pure, the clear, where art becomes an element in itself through immaculacy, something flawless and crystalline, unpremeditated and free; but as long as he remained director he was obliged to follow the routine of day-to-day affairs, the odious atmosphere of business, traps set by the malicious, the impenetrable undergrowth of human pettiness and triviality. But he tore a path through, hurled himself, surged forward, like a frenzied attacker towards this goal, which he knew to be beyond, on the outside, inaccessible and yet already lying within him: perfection. His whole life long he kept running, casting all else aside, knocking down, trampling anything which threatened to hold him up, he ran and ran, as if whipped by the terror of

33

not ultimately achieving perfection. In his wake resounded the hysterical shrieks of the aggrieved prima donnas, the groaning of the self-satisfied ones, the jeering of assorted mediocrities, the herd of conventional men, but he never turned back, he was oblivious to how the ranks of his persecutors swelled, he did not even feel the blows they rained down on him, for he stormed on and on until eventually he stumbled and fell. It was said he was inhibited by this resistance, that it undermined his life, but I don't believe it for a moment. Here was a man who absolutely needed resistance, he adored it, craved it; the bitter salt of everyday life only made him thirst the more for the eternal source. And in the holiday periods when he was relatively free of these afflictions, sequestered in Toblach or Semmering, he built his resistance through his work. Blocks of stone, mountains, bedrock of the spirit. Humanity's highest achievement, the second part of *Faust*, the song of the creative spirit 'Veni Creator Spiritus', he set before his musical will like a dam, then to flow over it with his creation. For battling with earthly things was his divine pleasure, bound as he was to the final day of accomplishment. The elemental in him loved the wrestling of free elements with the terrestrial world, he sought no respite; further, further, it drove him on to the only rest proper for the true mortal artist, which he finally earned with the 'Song of the Earth'.

Indescribable what we young people took from his example, for we sensed we too had the will within us to create art, witnessing that fiery spectacle in public there in the open. We were desperate to make some approach to him, submit ourselves to his will, but we were inhibited by a timidity, uncanny and enigmatic, like not daring to step to the crater's edge and gaze down into the molten embers. We never sought to force ourselves on him, for his mere being, his existence, or rather the consciousness of his being so close to us, at the heart of our common external world—this was already fortune enough for us. To have observed him on the street, in the coffee house, in the theatre, always from a distance, itself counted as a small victory, he was so much loved, so much revered. Even today his image is awake in me, as few others; I recall every time I encountered him from a distance. He was always different yet always the same, because he was perpetually enlivened by the ferocity of spiritual expression. I see him now in rehearsal: furious, twitching, shrieking, irritable, suffering from all number of inadequacies as if from physical pain; and seeing him once absorbed in a jovial conversation on the street, this too was elemental, the childlike cheerfulness that Grillparzer ascribes to Beethoven (and certain of whose grainy lines have found their way into the symphonies). He was always carried away by an inner force, always animated by the whole. But most unforgettable is the final time I saw him, for I have never felt so keenly, with all the senses, the heroism of the man. I was travelling back from America and he happened to be aboard the same ship and he was dying, a dying man. Early spring was in the air, the crossing was gentle, the waves light on the sea, there were just a handful of us gathered together, Busoni made a gift to us, we few friends, of his music. We should have been in high spirits, but down below, somewhere deep in the bowels of the ship, he lay dying in his wife's arms, and we felt it like a shadow cast over our light-hearted day. Sometimes, when we laughed, someone would say, 'Mahler, poor Mahler!' and we fell silent. Down there he lay, the lost one, burning with fever, and only the tiny, bright flame of his life flickered up on deck in the open air: his child, carefree at play, blissful and unaware.

35

But we, we knew, sensed the grave beneath our feet. And then the landing at Cherbourg. In the tugboat which ferried us in, I finally saw him: he lay there, pale as one already in the grip of death, inanimate, with closed lids. The breeze had swept his greying hair to one side, his arched brow projected clearly and boldly, and below was that firm chin, where the power of his will sat. The withered hands lay folded on the blanket, for the first time I really saw him, the fiery one, enfeebled. But this silhouette, unforgettable, unforgettable! was set against a grey infinitude of sky and sea, immeasurable grief was in this gaze but also something transfigured by greatness, something that faded into the sublime, like music. I knew then that I had witnessed him for the last time. Emotion drew me close, diffidence held me back; from a distance I only had to gaze on him, as if in seeing him I could in some way be welcomed by him and be thankful. Ripples of muffled music drifted over me, I thought of Tristan, the wounds of death, the homecoming to Kareol, his father's castle, but this was more profound, more beautiful, more transfigured. I found the melody and the words in his work, long since created, but only at that moment fulfilled, the death-blessed godlike melody in the 'Song of the Earth', to the words, 'I will never wander into the distance… silent is my heart and awaits its hour.' Now they are as one to me, these almost spectral sounds and this vision, an image gone but never forgotten.

But when he was gone, he was not entirely lost to us. His presence had long been more than just external to us, it was deeply rooted in us, had grown, because experiences that reach into the heart have no more yesterday. He is alive in us today as much as ever; a thousand times I still feel his indelible presence. A conductor in a German city raises his baton. In his gesture, his whole manner, I sense Mahler, I know without even enquiring that he is a student of his work, that here the magnetism of his life rhythm remains creative beyond mere existence (as I might often hear the voice of Kainz in the theatre, clearly as if issuing from a mute breast). In the playing of some people something else radiates of him, in the humanly austere attitude of some of the youthful musicians his essence appears as only a forced reflection. But his presence emerges most powerfully in the opera itself, in the quieter parts as much as the louder, in the tensed or relaxed house; like a fluid its essence has penetrated these walls that no exorcism can expunge. The decor may have faded, the orchestra is not what it was, but in a few performances—above all in *Fidelio*, *Iphigenia* and *The Marriage of Figaro*—I sometimes feel through Weingartner's idiosyncratic overpainting, through the thick, dusty layer of indifference which Gregor has laid over this precious possession, through all the webs of decay, something of his forcefulness of design, and involuntarily my gaze falls on the conductor's podium and thinks to see him there. Somewhere he is still present in this house, through the rust and rubble the pure glow of his nature still persists, as the last dying embers in the ashes. Even here, where he created in the transitory, where he merely made sounds and souls vibrate in the air, even here, where the motion of his labours has now ceased, a trace of his shade lingers, becomes a shadow itself and in the beautiful, the perfected, we still sense his presence. I am aware that I am no longer able to attend his operas any more with the required openness, my feeling in this space is too corrupted by remembrance and comparison serves to diminish the pleasure. Like every great passion, it has made us all unjust.

So his demon truly worked its genius on us, a whole generation. The others who now approach him remain estranged from his biographical portrait, can only adore that which has sublimated itself from the music in its strange fieriness, they can never know his whole being. If Mahler's work already sounds like something wrought from the ephemeral, from the highest stratum of German art, we cannot forget how he moulded his immortal vision out of the earthbound. They know only the essence, the scent of his being, while we know the glowing colour that enshrouded this chalice. An image from this time, a bridge of words back to those days, has surely been constructed in the beautiful book by Richard Specht (*Gustav Mahler*, Berlin, Schuster and Löffler, 1914) which everyone would benefit from reading, because it impresses without being over-reverential, it is familiar without breaking confidence, eschewing the formulaic, a living and first blossoming, already bound like a testament, but grateful only for an experience, that of Gustav Mahler. Here too we find the rhythm of those perfect evenings and the master's will to present the whole, immaculate, as if prematurely to bind everything together.

Whenever I open it, the lost takes on new life: I see an evening from the past, voices well up, images greet me, the ephemeral again becomes experience, and always I sense it, the living, and within it the will from which everything flowed and into which once more everything merged. It is a grateful hand that guides you and I feel grateful to that hand, because this author draws you closer to the mystery of Mahler. And where the words of the book no longer lead, but merely accompany— for how could you interpret music other than through poetry, which itself is only music, beatifically transformed—this epoch has finally awakened and assists with the work. The songs of Mahler, they now resound on their own terms, his symphonic works are fully realized, and now in these first days of spring the people of Vienna crowd around him. In the same hall where he was shown the door his work has forced its way back in, he now lives among us as in former times. His will has been fully consummated and there is a singular pleasure in experiencing here and now this resurrection of the dead.

And he is resurrected, Gustav Mahler, here in our midst, almost the last city of the German language to greet the master once more. The signs of the trappings of a classic may still be missing, the honorary grave is yet denied him, still no street proudly bears his name, the bust awaits to be sculpted—even that by Rodin, who in vain attempted to capture this fiery nature in rigid bronze—there is nothing in the foyer of the house he inspired like no other and made the true spiritual emblem of the city. Still they hesitate and prevaricate. But one stage has thankfully been reached, the despisers and abusers have disappeared, crawled away into the shadowy corners of shame, and the filthiest and most cowardly indulge in mendacious admiration. The crucifiers of yesterday today cry 'Hosanna!' and anoint the torn garment of his glory with myrrh and spices. Gone are the malicious tongues of yesteryear, none wants to admit to being among them. For the haters and hunters are so unproductive that they take fright when their own hatred bears no fruit. Chaos and discord—of opinions as much as people—that is their nefarious world, but they are quick to fall silent wherever an indomitable will creates its order and unbendingly strives for pureness of unity. For the great creative powers are mightier than the day, the hour, and each word of malice pales in the face of the work that is crafted by the will.

MEMORIES OF
EMILE VERHAEREN

(1917)

These pages of gratitude and loving memory were dictated in the midst of the global tempest of 1916, following the crushing news of Verhaeren's death.

They could not be published openly then, for in that period even the intellectual life of warring peoples had to be repressed. Anyone who wished to commemorate a Belgian subject would have caused offence to the overriding sensibility, or rather the absurdity of the moment.

That is why in 1917, away from the prying eyes of the censor, I had a limited number of copies printed for just a few selected friends. All justified my confidence in them. For that I am grateful. None of these copies have entered general circulation. My book was a requiem behind closed doors, a death vigil for a friend within an intimate circle.

But today, on the tenth anniversary of this day of grief, it may now be unveiled, this secret portrait of a venerated man, and without reticence, without amendment, neither in the sentiment, nor in the words. Perhaps, then, those who love the poet might refresh the consecration of that love by casting an eye over his life.

STEFAN ZWEIG
26th November 1926

I N THE THIRD YEAR of the war, just one of thousands of deaths, Emile Verhaeren departed us, and by means of the very machines of whose beauty he sang, torn apart like Orpheus by the Maenads. At some distance from this hour and his departure, fate has compelled me to recall the absurd and catastrophic destiny of a time when language suddenly became a frontier between peoples, the homeland a prison, where it was a crime not to see as an enemy those connected to you by the veins of spiritual consonance and intimate friendship. Excepting hate, all feelings, generosity, charity, pity, were expressly prohibited by the state; but grief, which dwells in the innermost depths of the soul, who can chase that out? And the memories, how can they ever hold back those sacred floods which in warm waves overflow the heart? The present might destroy our senseless world, perhaps the future might even darken and cast a shadow, but the past remains inviolable to all and her loveliest days shine forth like candlelight into the darkness of our own days, and onto these pages, where I write in Verhaeren's memory and for my own consolation.

It is for myself alone that I write these pages and for friends chosen from among those he knew and loved. I have already tried to show in a major biographical work his significance as a poet and a literary phenomenon. That work is freely available

43

for anyone to read in German, French or English. But for these memories, which are so personal, I do not seek the participation of a nation which, at the decisive hour of his life, he perhaps perceived as an enemy, but that of the community of the spirit for which all hostility is an aberration and hate an absurdity. For myself and his inner circle, I seek to paint the picture of a man so intimately fused with my own life that I cannot properly present his being without feeling as if my own life is irrevocably interwoven with his.

I must have been twenty years of age when I first made his acquaintance. He was the first great poet I had got to know on a personal level. At that time, the spark of poetry was already within me but it was tentative, like flickers of lightning across the sky of the soul: I was still uncertain whether I myself was a genuine elect of the Word, or merely had a hankering to be so; and most of all I wanted at last to encounter a real poet, face to face, soul to soul, someone who would set an example and act as a decisive force. From books I had developed a deep affection for poets: they seemed particularly alluring across distance and in death; I knew a few poets of our own time; but close up they proved disappointing and there was something rather unsavoury about the nature of their existence. There was really no one in my milieu at that time whose life might serve as an example, whose experience might guide me, whose concordance between nature and work could help me to assemble the still-uncertain forces bound up within me. In biographies I encountered countless examples of such poetical-human unity, but I was already aware even then that every law of life, every inner form of life has its foundation in life lived, of knowledge gained through experience and examples studied from life.

By way of experience I was far too young; as for prospective role models, I sought them unconsciously rather than consciously. Admittedly, the poets of our time came to our city, even entered my life. One evening in Vienna I saw Liliencron, surrounded by adoring friends, drowned in applause; there he sat at a table amidst the throng, trapped between people and words, so that in the mêlée his own were somehow lost. I shook the hand of Dehmel once in a crowd, snatched at the greeting of this one or that. But never was I able to get properly close. Clearly, to get to know some of them more intimately I would have to draw nearer, to force the issue, but a certain timidity prevented me, a reticence which later I recognized as the secret and happy law of my existence: that I should not actively seek something, for at the right time it will make itself known. What formed me did not come about through my own desire, through my active will, but always as a result of grace and fate; and so then did this wonderful being, who suddenly and at the most propitious moment entered my life, to form the spiritual constellation of my youth.

Today I realize how deeply indebted to him I am, but I'm not sure I can translate the gratitude I feel into words. I don't mean to say that this feeling of obligation refers to the literary influence of Verhaeren upon my work, but rather that such gratitude is addressed to that master of life personally, who bestowed on my youth the first impression of truly human values, who at each moment of his life taught that only a complete man can be a great poet, and thus with artistic fervour possessed an indelible faith in the poet's potential for a certain humanistic purity. Excepting the beloved, fraternal figure of Romain Rolland, never in all my later years has anyone shown me more clearly the sublime essence of the poet, nor exhibited that pure oneness of nature and virtue, than Verhaeren, the living being I love and to whom, now taken from us, I make it my sacred duty to pay tribute.

Verhaeren's work had fallen into my hands at an early stage. At first I thought this was by chance, but for a long time now I have been convinced that I owe this encounter to one of those coincidences which are in all human judgements in life the true and perhaps sole requirement issuing from the inner being. At that time I was still attending high school, I had just learnt French and perfected the language through translation and a then still-unrefined poetic imagination. In those days I had somewhere one of Verhaeren's early collections, published in only three hundred copies by Lacomblez in Brussels, which had long been something of a rarity for bibliophiles. It was one of the first books by the Belgian poet, and this Belgian was himself a stranger in the wider literary world. Over and again, so as to appreciate the creative coincidence, I must remind myself that Verhaeren's true work was then only just evolving, so it was more a mystical tendency ungrounded in reality that propelled me towards this unknown poet. Some of the poems stirred me and, employing my still-ungainly word craft on them, I, a mere seventeen-year-old, penned a missive to the poet seeking permission to publish them. The answer in the affirmative, preserved to this day, came from Paris; its postmark, showing a now-distant date, attests to the passage of time. Nothing linked me to him then, but I retained the name and the letter, which to my great astonishment I discovered many years later and which were proof to me that what I sought with the powers of a clear-sighted consciousness had been boyishly triggered unconsciously half a decade before.

In Vienna, the turn of the century was a momentous period richly endowed with spirit. As a student I was too young to take an active part, but it lingers in my memory as an epoch of renewal when suddenly, as if on an invisible breeze, the aroma and presentiment of strange and great art, a message from unseen lands, was borne into our old-fashioned city. The Secession experienced its pivotal years of activity and continued to flourish; and in their exhibitions the Belgians, Constantin Meunier, Charles van der Stappen, Fernand Khnopff and Laermans, enthralled us, used as we were to smaller-scale works, with their monumental forms. Belgium, the little country between languages, bewitched my imagination; I began to fall for its literature, to love Charles de Coster, whose *Ulenspiegel* I recommended in vain to all the German publishers for a decade. Barely out of school, I did the same for Camille Lemonnier and his Rubens-like novels, so intoxicated as they were with life. My first vacation trip took me there. I saw the sea, the cities and wished also to see those for whose work I felt such deep devotion. But it was summer, a sweltering August in 1902, the people had fled Brussels, whose asphalt melted beneath a febrile sun. Of those I sought to meet there was only Lemonnier, a delightful, obliging character whose memory I cherish and gratefully preserve. Not satisfied with his presence alone, he wished to offer me introductions to all the artists who meant something to me. But how to get hold of them, where to find them?

The whereabouts of Verhaeren, whose intimacy I would covet above all, were unknown. Maeterlinck had long since upped sticks from his Flemish home. No one, no one at all was around! But Lemonnier did not give in; he wanted me at least to see his paternal friend Meunier engrossed in his work, and Van der Stappen, his brotherly comrades. Only now do I understand what his gentle insistence would mean for me, for that hour with Meunier constitutes an imperishable possession and that with Van der Stappen one of the most significant of my life. I will never forget the day with Van der Stappen. The journal of that time has unfortunately been lost to me, but I don't have need of it for those hours are engraved on my mind as if with the sharp edge of a diamond, and what is possessed will never be forgotten.

One morning I made a pilgrimage to the rue de la Joyeuse Entrée, beyond the Cinquantenaire, and found Van der Stappen, the little amiable *flamand* with his full-figured Dutch wife, whose natural hospitality Lemonnier's friendly letter had possibly enhanced. I wandered with the master into the stone forest of his works. The *Monument à l'Infinie bonté*, which he had been creating for years and which he would never complete, stood impressively monumental at the centre and was surrounded by a rigid circle of single groupings, luminous marble, dark bronze, moist clay and burnished ivory. That amiable morning hour shone bright and clear and became ever more cheerful and lively through the spoken word. There was much talk of art and literature, of Belgium, of Vienna; the animated cordiality of these two soon banished all my timidity. Unashamedly I told them of my pain and disappointment at not meeting in Belgium those poets of the French language I esteemed above all others, and that I would not shy away from a further journey if there was the slightest prospect of encountering Verhaeren. But no one knew where he was; he had departed Paris, but not yet arrived in Brussels; there was simply no one who could tell me where he was to be found. I confessed my regret at having to return home along with my great devotion, which seemed destined to remain so only in word and at a distance.

Van der Stappen gave a little covert smile as I said this, his wife also smiled, and they exchanged glances. I sensed a secret acquiescence between them kindled by my words. At first I was puzzled and somewhat concerned that I might have said something they had taken offence to. But soon I realized they were not annoyed at all and we resumed our conversation. Another hour passed with me none the wiser, and when I made ready to take my leave they seemed to resist and motioned that I must stay at the table, that I must on no account leave. And again, the same little smile flashed from eye to eye. I felt that if there was some secret here it was at the least a benign one, so I delayed my intended trip to Waterloo and stayed in the bright, friendly, hospitable house.

Soon midday arrived. We were already sat in the dining room on ground-floor level next to the street, as is the way in those little Belgian houses, and from the room we could look out through the windows' coloured panes. Suddenly a shadow stopped before the window. A finger knocked at the coloured glass and at the same moment the bell was rung brusquely. 'Here he is!' exclaimed Frau van der Stappen, and rose to her feet. I had no idea what she meant, but the door opened and in he came with that determined heavy step, fraternally embracing the Van der Stappens: Verhaeren. At first look I recognized his incomparable face from pictures and photographs.

Now that their friendly little secret was out, Van der Stappen and his wife no longer smiled in a clandestine manner but gave full rein to their gaiety, like children rejoicing in their success. As was the custom, it was on this particular day that Verhaeren would pay them a visit, and when they heard I had sought him everywhere in vain they had made a pact to divulge nothing and to surprise me with his presence.

And there he now stood before me, smiling too at the successful prank played. For the first time I felt the firm grip of his nerve-filled hand, for the first time I took in his clear, benevolent look. As always he entered the house as if brimming with new experiences and enthusiasms. Even as he fell on the food, he was already in full flow. He had been with friends in a gallery and still burned feverishly with this hour spent in their company. He always returned home from every place and every thing enriched by random experience, and this enthusiasm had become a divine custom; like a flame from his lips and marvellously, with keen gestures, he was able to draw the word, to reveal the object of his attention through rhythm and form. With the first word he reached right into the person, for he himself was open and accessible to every new thing, never negative, always prepared to embrace all. He launched himself with his entire being, so to speak, out beyond himself, and hundreds of times I have seen this overwhelming, stormy impact of his being on others. Of me he still knew nothing, yet he was already filled with gratitude for my sake, he already took me into his confidence simply because he had learnt that I had some connection to his work. And spontaneously, before that powerful impact of his being, all sense of shyness left me. I felt free as never before in the presence of this curious, open man. His gaze, strong, steely and clear, unlocked the heart.

The meal was over quickly. Even today, after a year and a day, I picture the three of them standing there together, as my gaze rises up to embrace them: Van der Stappen, small, with a ruddy complexion, exuberant, like a Bacchus by Jordaens, Madame van der Stappen, large and maternal, joyful out of the joy of others, then he, with his wolf-like appetite, with his splendid gesticulations fuelling the passion of his narrative; I see these three people from the past, who had such fraternal love for one another, and in whose words a consummate blitheness dwelt. Never before in Vienna had I known such a sphere of deep inner feeling and well-ripened jocundity as at this little table, and I experienced a rapture to the core of my being whose urgency was almost painful. The glasses chinked one more time, the armchairs were cleared and Verhaeren and Van der Stappen embraced. Then it was over.

I wanted to say my farewells, despite the beauty of the moment. But Van der Stappen held me back and for the second time confided a secret. He was just now working to fulfil a long-held desire by creating a bust of the poet. It was already far advanced and was due to be completed that very day; I was warmly invited by all to attend the grand finale. My presence, Van der Stappen insisted, was a gift of fortune, for he required someone to converse with the restless model while he was sitting, so that his face would come alive and he would not be unduly fatigued by holding the pose for a long period. I was to talk about my projects, of Vienna, of Belgium, anything I wished, until the work was completed. Then we could all celebrate this great accomplishment together. Do I need to add how overjoyed I was to be present, when a great master was creating the portrait of another great man?

The work commenced. Van der Stappen disappeared. The elegant redingote, which (with the corresponding embonpoint) somehow recalled President Fallières, had vanished when he returned. Before us stood a simple worker in a white smock, sleeves rolled up showing muscles like those of a butcher. The bourgeois placidity had drained from his features, and like the god-smith Vulcan, flaming-red with the ardour of his will, he stepped forward, restless with impatience to set to work, and led us into the workshop. Deep and bright was the room which we had passed through before, in cheerful discourse. But now the figures seemed more sober and the white marble statues stood silent like so many stony thoughts in the room. Before us a block stood upon a pedestal. Van der Stappen loosened the damp cloths from the clay. The face of Verhaeren emerged, so familiar with those violent angular forms, but ultimately alien, as if composed only from memory. Van der Stappen advanced a step, inspected his work then Verhaeren, and for a full minute his gaze wandered from one to the other. Then he stepped back decisively. His eyes gleamed, his muscles tightened. The work began.

Goethe once remarked to Zelter that to properly know a great work of art one must have seen it evolve. In the same way, a human face is not fully known from the first encounter. One must have observed it grow from childhood to maturity and then give way to old age. Or we can see it as a form of reproduction, in which the established element is disassembled into its essential parts, form into its proportions; comparing line by line, trait by trait in their incremental existence, we can follow the new construction of art. In these two hours with Van der Stappen, Verhaeren's face was as if sculpted into my soul and ever since it has been part of me, as if it were of my own blood. Of the many hundreds of encounters with him since, I always see him as I saw him then in this creative hour so many years ago, the lofty brow already furrowed sevenfold with lines from the years of misfortune and, drooping over them, the heavy, rust-brown locks. Bony and hard the structure of the face, severely embraced with brownish, masculine, wind-tanned skin; the chin prominent, hard and rock-like; violent and massive, threatening and almost hostile the low-hanging Vercingetorix moustache, shadowing the lower lip with a tragic melancholy. But all this hard virility, how wonderfully gently it was resolved by the steel-grey gaze—colour of the sea—clear and open, knowing and contented with knowing, glinting in the reflection of the beloved light! Nervousness dwelt in those hands, those slender, gripping, delicate yet powerful hands, where the veins pulsed powerfully beneath the thin skin. Yet the whole force of his will was there in the broad, rugged shoulders, above which the small, nervous bony head seemed almost too small: only when he strode forth was his strength made apparent.

Seeing the bust today, I feel Van der Stappen never realized a greater triumph than in the work of that hour—I know how consummate it is and how true. The head inclines a little, not through weariness, but to listen more attentively, not in the face of life, but for life, to grasp more profoundly its knowledge. When I gaze at it, I know this is not a portrait but a memorial, a document of poetic greatness, the monument of an imperishable power. But at that time, in that strange hour, it was nothing but a soft, moist tone of the spatula striking and the finger smoothing, this work was only a feeling towards, a preparatory assessment and comparing, at that time he was still animated, and in the pauses he beamed with the breath of the conversation, and he listened with that impressive strength of his inexhaustible sympathy. Barely noticing that dusk had descended, master Van der Stappen never tired. More and more often he would take a step back from his sculpture, allowing his gaze to pass between the living subject and its image, which even now began to become a living thing; less and less did his hands now stray to the created work. Gradually his fixed gaze grew more serene, his eye lost the restlessness, the flickering spark, once more only now he handled the clay, casting a glance over and across. Then he untied the apron, groaned deeply and with a hint of regret, almost a sigh more than a word, he breathed 'Finished'. Verhaeren rose to his feet. He thumped his approval upon the shoulder of the little stout man, panting and breathless, yet smiling before his work, and now he was no longer the Vulcan in his smithy but the proud bean-king of Jordaens; how they laughed together. A geniality as between lads now sprang up between these two men, on both of whose hair and beards a touch of snow shone. For the first time I sensed here a brighter, more liberated humanity than I had ever known between artists, whom I had always viewed as solicitous, jealously safeguarding their 'business'; and the feeling winged its way to me almost mystically that I too could gain this freedom and security for my own life in the midst of art. But awe had me by the throat and I sensed the yawning distance. Yet some part of my being had already attached itself to this poet, and as I took his hand, so genially proffered amidst the farewells and promises of a speedy reunion, I realized he had captured my heart. I was already aware that it was a gift, a great gift, to be able to serve such people, and through a murky sense I gauged that my will and destiny was to devote myself to his work. Heartily grateful, I took Van der Stappen's hand and left.

It was already turning dark in the high room. As I turned back at the door, I saw in the shadows, white and tall, *L'Infinie bonté* and Verhaeren there before it, his hand resting against the bright stone. It was only later, much later, that I knew that this work, which for its completion only lacked the great supporting figure, was properly realized in this very moment, with Verhaeren leaning against the block of stone, and to my eyes it appeared like a symbol, his soul merged with it.

From his work I had now discovered a real poet, and my first inclination was to rediscover the poet in his work. But if

54

I say 'Verhaeren's work', I have to remind myself how little the former equated with that later huge achievement which is admired and revered the world over today. For the foundations had barely been laid, only those Parnassian works of *Les Flamandes* and *Les Moines* were known, and the fiery visions of *Les Villes tentaculaires* and *Les Villages illusoires* were only recently forged. But there was still darkness, chaos and fiery light enough in them and the dawn of goodness and clarity, that incomparable ascension to purity which became the greatness and timeless thought of his art. And now, as I look back, I am fully conscious of the joy it has brought me to witness this ascent close up, from book to book, even poem to poem, often absorbed one at a time, or read aloud on quiet evenings, to see born a fragment of immortality at the heart of our epoch. What today might be passed over as desiccated literary history I inhaled as a living fragrance, the breath and waxing of this unfading blossom nourished through fifteen years of friendship and familiarity, and what today is merely marketed as a book, passed from hand to hand, was known to me in torment, secrecy and creative form. I recall too how philanthropic I felt with all my will towards the still-unconsummated work, how my confidence in the man, in what was shapeless and nameless, was yet to be proven, and how back then I spoke his name into the void, a name that has now become commonly accepted in the literary canon! And with such a memory I learn to give thanks for my youth.

But gladly I launched myself into these labours. A few translated poems I could now send on to the master, and the return letters told of his joy. His fame began slowly and my promotion of his name also, but I knew that in spite of everything nothing was more admirable than that time, when the modest joys and successes were still great ones, for out of what seemed like an exercise in futility came the purest human feeling.

A few years went by. I was absorbed by my own milieu, but letters of greeting went back and forth between us. At first only a scattering, religiously preserved in tiny envelopes which were soon insufficient, then they became hundreds bound together by bands. I would love to read them over and over, to arrange them chronologically, sift through them and properly savour them, but alas I never get the chance. And even now, knowing that no page in his hand will ever be borne my way again and that the final letter was the final for all time, the bond will never loosen and I shall endeavour to restore to life that which has passed away for ever. For my mind guards itself against the knowledge of loss and with an anxious and pious reserve I eschew the cemetery of words. The letters of that time long past and their extinct feeling lie buried for ever.

So the years went by. I completed my studies, the world lay free and open before me and asked that I advance and learn about it. The first year of my new-found freedom I gave to Paris. I arrived late in the evening, and from a café on the boulevards I sent word to him. Of the many plans for my new life, he was the first in line and the most important. The next morning, barely awakened, I found a little blue envelope in front of the door to my room: he would be waiting for me at noon in his home at Saint-Cloud.

From Gare Saint-Lazare I went out past Passy, with its hundred belching factories, and on to the more peaceful, verdurous outer suburbs. From the Parc de Montretout I saw the city laid out, Paris almost invisible in the damp haze of a wet October day, only the grey slate pencil of the Eiffel Tower writing its name upon the soft sky. Two streets from the park I found it, a suburban row of small, red-brick cottages with six or ten windows apiece. A place for pensioners, better-off workers, officials and folk of lesser means, those who craved silence and a little greenery, suburban civilians, uninquisitive, quiet, reserved types. Paris the violent and elemental: hard to imagine it was nearby. Down there was the wave and here the quiet beach.

Then to the little house, two high wooden steps, a plain door without a name, a simple bell that I rang a little shyly, then for the first time, but how often since, he came to the door with a heartfelt hand, with that spontaneous joy of reception that came from the very depths of his ever-open humanity. Geniality was all for him, it was enough to be in his presence and at the first gesture it sprang forth. At the first press of his hand, at his open gaze, at his first utterance, you could sense his sincerity right to the heart.

How small this dwelling, how simple, how middle-class! No poet I knew had such a spartan home. A front room and three more behind it, every one tiny and crammed to the ceiling. There was no space left in the room, furnishings filled it, the walls were lined with books and colourful pictures, all illuminated by the yellowed bindings of French editions. A Rysselberghe bursting with colours, a Carrière with dark overtones and ten or twenty other canvases by friends, crowded frame by frame, and there at the centre of the room the table laid out for the guest with simple rustic dishes. A red wine in the carafe sparkled like a fiery flower.

Next door, the study, books and more books and pictures along the wall, two low chairs for conversation, a wooden table with a colourful spread, a student's inkwell, a cheap ashtray, stationery in a cigar box, and that was it, the work desk of a poet. No artificial contrivance, no typewriter, no tapes, no shelves, no telephone, nothing which smacked of the office, which makes the working space of the writers of today so desperately resemble that of a business. No comfort, no luxury, nothing unnecessary, nothing overbearingly artistic, everything modest and petty-bourgeois, tasteful but without obtrusiveness, frugal without distraction. A tiny world in whose silence a great one would prosper.

Soon we sat at the table and dined in good cheer. Simple and tasty food. In the Flemish tradition as head of the table, Verhaeren, armed with skewer and knife, skilfully cut the meat into slices and Madame Verhaeren smiled warmly at this mastery, of which, as she affirmed, he was prouder than his poems. Then coffee arrived. Frau Verhaeren waved to us and disappeared.

Now I sat alone with him in his little room, cigar and pipe smoke wove a light cloud around the books, we chatted, he read some poems, it was homely in that little room. Every word here took on earnestness and resonance. The hours flew by on wings and it was evening before you knew it. At last I took my leave from that first day in his house. He showed me to the door and once again I felt the warmth of his hand, and from the window he waved to me on the street, 'À bientôt!'

The October evening was marvellous. I was still brimming with conversation and a sense of rapture. I was too overcome by all I had experienced to allow the railway to disturb the miraculous, almost floating sensation of well-being. So instead I wandered down to the Seine to take one of the swift little boats back to the city. The sun had gone down now, the red lamps glowed on the steamers, the city had sunk into darkness and at the same time gleamed with artificial light. The boat sped me quickly from the countryside into the dusking sea of Paris. The

Trocadero, the Eiffel Tower steadily loomed above the droning breath of the metropolis with all its confused cacophony. The night of that city of cities glowed wonderfully, and on this first day in Paris I was fortunate enough to have learnt that both one and the other ends of life share equal strength: the masses and the lone, great, beneficent man.

How often, how many countless times did I see him there in those little rooms, and how different was it back then? How many new and familiar faces did I gaze into at the narrow table, for these modest rooms were seldom lacking a guest, yet saw only a handful at a time. There was always some kind of intellectual activity, flooding in from all shores of the world. Youthful French poets, old comrades, Russians, Englishmen, Belgians, some with names that rang out, others whose existence was fleeting; how many passed through there, filled the hours with the breath of their novel presence in the humanistic atmosphere of that room, so dominated by Verhaeren's vital, earnest and always creative persuasiveness. According to custom one would come just before the table was set, before the evening meal, because the morning was naturally a time for work. Always an early riser, Verhaeren sat down to breakfast around six or seven o'clock and then remained at his desk till ten o'clock. The remainder of the day was given over to life, to reading, to trips, to friends. Around eleven o'clock, armed with his heavy cane, he wandered like a rustic pilgrim into Paris, to look at paintings, to dine with friends or just roam aimlessly about the city, to surrender himself to the random tide of the masses which he so loved. His daily work was already done and, like a robber baron seeking adventures beyond his castle, he set off in carefree mood into the city to seize on prey in order to satiate his immense curiosity. He trudged the streets for hours on end, took in small exhibitions or, always a welcome guest, stopped by to visit friends, strolled through the museums for the tenth or twentieth time that year, rode the top deck of the omnibus amidst the foam and spray of the city, or tramped with heavy tread over the asphalt of the boulevards.

Once I encountered him on the *quai* of the Seine, by the Palais de L'Académie; I recognized him up ahead by that heavy way of walking, which recalled a country labourer plodding behind the hand plough, and, curious, I took a particular pleasure in not greeting him right away so I could be attentive to his wanderings. He paused at the *bouquinistes*, leafed through books, walked on, halted at a landing stage where a heavy tractor laden with fruit and vegetables was being loaded. He stood there for a good half-hour, entranced, every detail interested him: the muscles stretched on the back of a labourer shouldering sacks, the cranes with their soft screeches, the groaning of the load rising from the belly of the ships and being placed so carefully, almost tenderly on the stone ramp. He conversed with the workers so naturally, quite deliberately, out of the deep curiosity of his being, which sought to understand all about every element of existence. For half an hour he remained there with this extraordinary fanatical curiosity, which was as it were both animate and inanimate, then he trudged back over the bridge to the boulevards. It was now that I approached him. He laughed when I said I had been spying on him and immediately began to recount all he had learnt; he was lucky, for he had recognized the dialect of his homeland when talking to one of the ship workers. We went to the Marchand de Vins, one of those little shops where you can dine simply and cheaply, and his memory was awakened to a vision of ships along the canals and rivers of France all ablaze with light; he was already glowing to the core with the will to set to work. It was on such promenades that many of his great poems came into being and the countless little details in his verses would have been inconceivable without the irresistible curiosity which led him through life, a life eternalized by individual experiences, whose ultimate abundance came in the wonderfully expanded vision of a unified world found in his verses.

Late in the evening, drunk with dialogue and image, he travelled back to Saint-Cloud, always in third class, among the workers and clerks with whom he loved to converse. At home, the silence of the small room and the table with its spread; sometimes a friend might be waiting for him there, but soon the paraffin lamp would go out in his room. A miraculous monotony of external existence harboured an infinite variety of activity. The day began with work, then gave way to life, sank back once more in the evening to quiet conversation or silent communion with books. All that constitutes a quintessential social life had no place in his compulsive, regulated existence; he never attended the salons, formal dinners, premières, nor did he visit the editorial offices. He knew nothing of Saint-Germain, the same old rehearsals, the races, the festivals, which for the stranger seduced by novels seemed to be the only true Paris. The intensity of people, the wide, streaming streets, the mystical, tender sunsets on the Seine—that for him was Paris, not the constant bustle of gatherings and events, the world of wit and fashion. He searched for the core, the mysterious and intoxicating, not the sparkling ornaments of this city. Through his life there I first came to understand the secret of this most productive city in the world, which seems to be all about fleeting pleasure and surface appearance and where, in cramped garrets, in the suburbs and in odd little bourgeois rooms, the decisive works are wrought. Thus each evening this little room in Saint-Cloud, a world in itself, caught the rhythm of those others in all their sound and clamour and set about transforming the whole into poetry and music. Here the force of the Paris masses fed the solitary work, and the solitary work in turn created the image of the spirit of the great metropolis.

This was the life he had chosen: Paris, the most powerful, the most vivid, the most open and yet the most inscrutable city in Europe. He had surely selected it as a place to settle due to the cosmopolitan, contemporary nature of his being, for he loved its heightened energy and unquenched atmosphere, he wanted above all to be here in the city of cities. Half the year, from autumn till spring, he resided in Paris, seemingly at the city's outer limits, but in terms of perception at its very heart. This half-year he was a citizen of the world, a modern, European man working at the cutting edge. The other half of the year he was an ordinary Fleming, a native son, a hermit, a peasant who belonged only to nature. Anyone who encountered him in Paris knew only one half of his life, the spiritual, the intellectual, the European. But only he who experienced him on this patch of home soil, in his garden, in his little cottage, could claim to know him. Anyone who wanted to get to know him properly, when faced with the poles of his double life, would have to meet him in the calm of his native fields, in Caillou-qui-Bique.

Caillou-qui-Bique is not a town, nor a village or hamlet; there is not even a railway station and even the most intrepid would not find their way there without his amiable helping hand. The nearest station was Angreau, and this tiny halt listed in the guide was in fact merely an overturned goods wagon with a map affixed to its side next to the branch line to Roisin, at which some simple peasant will, without even bothering to alight, simply toss down the post sack. This little place is at the far ends of the earth when viewed through the complexity of the rail timetable, yet in truth it lies only four hours from Brussels, London, Cologne and Paris, a point at the heart of Europe lost in the invisible.

This backwater, with its curious name, owes its existence to an overhanging rock in the vicinity, a tiny natural wonder which could only occur in these flatlands. This scattering of four or five dwellings is located in a far-flung corner of Belgium, right up against the French border. From the neighbouring town of Angre, one road goes to Quiévrain and the other to Valenciennes, and you can afford the modest luxury of setting out at midday in Belgium, spending the afternoon in France and returning home to Belgium in the evening. This ease of crossing borders favours smugglers, who are active all over with their tobacco and lace, their dogs laden with small packages, hunting through the darkness, but the gendarmes with their rifles are well aware of this. As peaceful as Wallonia appears, there is a certain air of romantic intrigue to its clandestine frontiers. Hundreds upon hundreds of stories Verhaeren must have recounted on this subject, and found among his papers after his death was a prose drama about smugglers which he composed when he first settled in the area. But he never managed to complete it, deferring the work from year to year, and now this first attempt at a modern peasant tragedy (in the weighty, solid style of our master dramatist) will remain for ever a fragment.

This, then, is a lost corner, and without the gracious compass of his guidance, without the magnetism of his being, the stranger would never find his way there. You must go first from Brussels to Mons, pass the high-walled prison where Verlaine spent two years and where he wrote *Sagesse*, in Mons you change to a local train and then take another which is so slow that a bicycle could easily overtake it. But this journey, slow as it is, and long-winded, is for this very reason all the more beautiful and memorable. Barely have we left Mons when from the clod-filled fields the peaks rise up, conical summits of the coal chimneys, the slag heaps, oppressive and dark beneath the sky, and the wind that blows in from the Belgian coast damp and salty here becomes rather greyish and acrid. As if through a murky blanket, an extraordinary world is here laid out: the Borinage, the mining region, the black earth, whose proletarian figures Constantin Meunier has turned to stone in his sculptures. Again and again the train grinds to a halt because one workers' town crowds in on the next, a hundred black chimneys exhale their black breath and by night their fiery tongues push into the eternally gloomy sky. The whole tragic, unprepossessing and yet grandiose modern world is happening just an hour's journey away. But soon it all fades like a maleficent dream, luminous and pristine the clouds gleam over a clear sky, the houses glow red in the yellow fields, and with soft green the young forests rush up to the tracks. The landscape of Wallonia is fertile and festive. Impatiently you scan the timetable of the little station halt at Angre and finally Angreau.

And there he stands waiting to greet the guest, your hand feels the warm pressure of his and the kiss on the cheek. Dressed like a countryman in a soft corduroy suit, breeches, no collar to speak of and wooden clogs on his feet, he stands there amidst the trees, more like an American farmer or a worker of the land than a bourgeois type. With rustic staff in hand he strides cheerfully up the narrow mule path, his white dog, Mempi, ever faithful, leaps to and fro at his side. No road proper leads to his house, no cart track, only this narrow mule path, overgrown with exuberant greenery. For half an hour or so it goes on like this, crossing meadows and heaps, woods and hedgerows, sometimes passing a barn or farmhouse, where the country folk doff their caps revealing their straw-blond locks, greeting M. Verhaeren with respectful camaraderie. The land is lush and green, the meadows are sated with moist air, the cows lying there are white-spotted like the clouds, which scud restlessly across the sky from the sea. A grove slopes uphill, then the little house peeps out low down behind the front garden, a small fenced farmstead. Verhaeren unlatches the garden gate. We pass through. We are now in his house. But is this really a house? Not even a cottage, in fact, just a brick barn with a wooden roof, simple and unadorned, beautiful for the climbing embellishment of roses and greenery that are woven over the deep red of the brickwork. Six windows, or eight in all, blank and hung with white muslin, a mansard under the roof, a yard with clucking hens, a little garden with a few blazing sunflowers. Nearby there is a house, of course, a proper one-storey house with a little balcony, but that belongs to Laurent, the owner of Caillou-qui-Bique and is a homestead, dwelling and also a hostelry. On Sundays the neighbours come on their little wagons, sit on the narrow benches in the bower to drink the dull, warm Belgian beer, play an hour of skittles, and in recent years sneak through to the neighbour's house to catch a glimpse of the famous poet whom they have heard much about but so little read. Then the wagons are harnessed again, and an hour past sundown the house slips back into its idyllic silence. There are no strangers on weekdays, at most the priest or postman passes, otherwise there is only Laurent, the good-natured, broad-shouldered giant who toils in the fields during the day and, weary come evening, reads the newspaper behind his glass of beer or makes mischief with his good friend Verhaeren. On weekdays that divine peace from the first day of creation reigns.

Verhaeren discovered this world, the home of his greatest and most beautiful works, by accident. Years before, he had come there to rest and recuperate, lodging with Laurent at the inn. Soon he cherished the landscape for its silence and remoteness. He was tempted to remain there at a distance from the world, in this far-flung corner of his homeland, yet still near the centres of his spiritual existence: Paris, Brussels and the sea. He did not feel at home living in a rented room, but building a house seemed to him a burden and an obligation. Still, he prized freedom above all else, and so he agreed with Laurent that he should have the next-door barn, which was unused, and adapt it to his needs. The few rooms on the ground floor were converted into living accommodation, the attic into a bedroom and a wooden staircase was installed, and so this primitive, exemplary poet's residence slowly took shape, becoming the home of his last years and a place of pilgrimage for friends.

Here and only here was the poet entirely at home with himself. Here, when he was roaming around in a corduroy suit without a collar or tie, wearing clogs in all weathers, wind and rain, storm and sunshine, here he was inwardly free and open. Here he could escape the chance visits, the temptations and distractions, here he could listen to himself uninterruptedly, and whoever was received there as a guest did not touch his life in a fleeting sense, but themselves grew into the house, shared the daily table, the long hours and the silence. Here too, as in Paris, everything was simple and comfortable—the noble simplicity has few nuances, save for here—before the windows the soft green of murmuring foliage aroused calm, and the cockcrow announced the morning hour in place of the sirens of Paris. The garden which surrounded the house was quite small, and extended only five paces or so, but the land beyond belonged to anyone who wanted it. Meadows, forests and fertile fields were open however far one cared to roam. The notion of possession and of boundaries vanished here altogether in the wonderful sense of presiding solitude.

How tranquil, how full, how happy was the course of a day here! I myself was granted five summers and was ever grateful and content in Caillou-qui-Bique, and I know that for the first time during those summers I learnt the meaning of a life lived simply and the beauty it grants, for the first time I learnt from this model of a silent-sounding existence the deep law of harmony, in which every man must enter into communion with a landscape in order fully to enter into nature and the world. Here all was regularity and rest and in the midst of the unfilled, unaccountable, unbroken time, the quiet, cheerful flame of the day's work flared up into immortality! How long the day passed here, and yet at the same time how quickly did it fade. These five summers are lodged in my memory like a single blissful summer hour, and the concept of an idyll, which suggests something artificial and literary, was here crystal clear to me. In these hours Verhaeren was so close and safe, so secure and lost, so open and trusting that one rested and at the same moment stretched oneself further, for here was solitude and the world. In the evening, when we sat around the table and read to each other from books, poems that one loved or the other, they seemed somehow divine or supernatural, as if carried from a strange world into this little room; and yet in these same rooms, during those years, the works that spoke throughout Europe came into being. Oh, that quiet, the silence around the work, I still pensively listen for it many an hour, that quiet music of the hours where all vexation is absent. Never did I hear a squabble there, never a venomous word, a loud voice, never a shadow of mistrust in the softly luminous light of merriment that floated in the air. The mastery of life with a poet—here I experienced it for the first time, as never before and never again in my life.

Like a brook transparent and clear, the hours with their gentle music flowed there. At dawn the cock crowed and summoned you from bed, and you went to breakfast in slippers, often in shirtsleeves, then the postman arrived with letters that had travelled for three days and the newspapers of yesterday and before yesterday. But here, yesterday and tomorrow were not so tightly fastened to the day, here they lay both near and far at the same time, not forcefully tethered to the hour. On the white table waiting for breakfast lay eggs and milk in all varieties, home-baked fare, the only fruit from exotic climes being the brown cigar, whose smoke billowed about the conversation. Then it was work. It was the first law of the morning and seldom interrupted even on Sunday or a public holiday. But how light it was, how joyful, outside in the little pavilion, in the green shade under the sun amidst the many whispering voices of the countryside! At ten or eleven Verhaeren set out for his walk; usually he strolled across the fields, stick in hand, following the rhythm of his verse, his arms sometimes tracing the inner pathos of his creative vision. How often have I seen him so from afar, the broad-shouldered wanderer, walking through his poem, sending words on the wind he loved so, then returning home, flushed, radiantly cheerful, because somewhere he had managed to locate a line of verse and knotted a poem together to the very end. Lunch was brief. Everything was simple, mostly from the garden and the stable, the lush fruits of the earth, milk served in the most delicious ways, a thick side of meat which he cut himself. Usually one was alone with him, but sometimes a guest came who was gladly received and as gladly let go. The afternoon belonged to wandering. You could explore the surrounding forest or go to Angre, the nearby village, visit the local friends whom he loved so much, or sit down with the engraver Bernier and watch how with needle and pin he scored the plate, or to the lawyer, the pastor, the brewer, the printer, the blacksmith, or take the train to Valenciennes, discussing politics, agriculture, but never literature. When the rain came you could sit at home, write letters, read to each other from books, and then Verhaeren would reach into his published works and recite them, inflamed once more with the fire of the renewed word. Or you leafed through old letters, each one arousing memories of those first successes, the first challenges, and through those long, windy, rainy days I learnt so much about his life. In the evening the couple sat quietly together again, read a little, or he went over to play cards with Laurent at the counter by the kerosene lamp, like an old farmer who had fled to dry shelter out of the storm. By nine o'clock it was over, darkness fell, night, silence and sleep.

If his existence seemed petty-bourgeois in the city, then it seemed so too in the countryside. And yet this unpretentious, inconspicuous way of life was crucial to him so that he could align all his forces towards the metropolis, towards time or here towards nature and eternity. As he absorbed the city, bursting with ideas, with people, taking part in everything, so here he nourished himself for six months on silence and allowed his body to replenish with strength and vigour, and his works were part of the air and atmosphere of the countryside. Whereas in the city he pushed his nerves to the limit, here he granted them rest. Yet here too they were wonderfully awake, his senses, and the artist hearkened to everything around him. Like some gigantic mill, all the fructuous things of the rural world poured into him, grain by grain, detail by detail, to be ground on the millstone there into the finest, most poetic form. Only those who knew something of this place knew the miracle of how a landscape could truly enter a person. Every path and every flower of the garden, the holy seasons of the land and the quiet work of man, here everything was sublimated in individual lines of verse and made timeless. Whenever I read his idyllic poems, I see again the path around the garden, I see the roses blooming around the windows and feel the wind, drunk with the sea blowing over Flanders, and see him in the midst of it all, eternally in his house and in the fields.

So his life was divided up in this fashion. In the city and the country, in creation and rest, in presence and timelessness, because he always craved everything so intensely, in its unbroken state and at its most powerful. In the last decade of his life, this transition was as regulated as the year itself, perfectly balanced between Paris and Caillou. But in-between there was still that lost month: the hay-fever season of the first moment of spring. Then the landscape, so beloved, was turned into a physical agony, the increased sensitivity to the pollen transformed what for us is a mystifying, sweet intoxication of the senses—spring—into burning bodily pain. The eyes began to water, a leaden ring became clamped about his head, all the senses were in turmoil. So violently did the tempest of nature break upon his sensitive form. No medical solution—he had tried them all—could keep the hay fever at bay, the only means to resist was to flee the greenery, escape from the landscape. He always spent those months by the sea, whose powerful breath blows away the bursting blossoms of the flowers, or in that other sea of stone, which devours the breath of blossoms with dust and stink: the big city. This month of May was the most hated and most barren of his life. Verhaeren was either in Brussels on the fourth floor of an apartment building on the boulevard du Midi, a prisoner of his suffering, without strength to work, impatiently waiting for the summer proper. Or else he fled to the coast, which he had loved from childhood, but even there he never worked. 'La mer me distrait trop,' he always claimed. It was too overpowering for him in another sense, too much of a fantasy. He was utterly mesmerized by the ebb and flow of the waves, the winds and storms, he had too much passion for it, for this was his *Heimat*. The North Sea was to some extent an amalgamation of all that was required for his soul: the strength and sombreness, the aimless, disorderly power, the monumental, to which he felt eternally drawn; and how he loved this grey sea, all those grey guests of the north, the rain, the dusk, the storm, more than the colourful splendour of the south. Nowhere was he so at home as here and no beauty could ever replace the Flemish beauty. Once he had been in Italy, fascinated and yet tormented by the endlessly radiant sky, by the uniform beatitude of this for him too peaceful world, and when on the return to St Gotthard rain fell on the carriage for the first time he forced the window down and let the hard welts batter against his mane of hair and tanned skin. Nowhere did he feel so strong as by the sea, too strong, as he confessed, to shape anything. This month, the lost one, was not lost to him either, and that was the incomparable mastery of his life: everything finally transformed through enthusiasm into joy and possession.

This flight into nature and its urban counterpart: petty-bourgeois simplicity made this great, multifaceted and word-spanning life simple and humble like that of a peasant or a town-dweller. It freed him from material distress, but at the same time, through the saving of otherwise fruitlessly wasted energies, fuelled the vital and poetic power immeasurably. Never have I witnessed the sharing-out of one's true activities more marvellously in one being, and never have I seen the problem solved of finding completeness in one's work while at the same time being entirely open to people. Regular and harmonious as the inhaling and exhaling of breath was this exchange, and it lent his existence a wonderful, cheerful-sounding rhythm. But, enhanced by his natural geniality, he had the right distribution when it came to friendship. He adored having his friends over one by one, fully engaged, not in crowds, not in hurried hours, but in the most powerful expansion of their single being. Rarely was he really alone in Caillou, his desert of solitude. His close friends liked to come on pilgrimage and stay a week, and after this week they knew more about each other than after a hundred fleeting encounters, because they all grew into the house and into his life. And as his friends loved to live with him, so he loved to live with them. He hated inns and hotels with their attempts to uphold formalities which denied the soulful ambiance around the individual. If he was in Brussels for a few days he was usually to be found at Montald's, in Paris he sometimes resided with Carrière, or with Rysselberghe, in Liège he was with Nysten's, and my own little room in Vienna still thinks gratefully of the days he, the ever frugal, spent there. The need to indulge in trust was inestimable in him, brimming over into the corporeal, as he loved to engage with friends, thump them on the shoulders, and after any time apart familiar faces were greeted with hugs and kisses. Disgruntlements and petty estrangements never prevented his free and open heart from expanding, and his geniality in overlooking small mistakes became almost a passion.

Of course, such goodness could not exist without a level of encroachment. He had known this for years and he permitted himself a smile. It was in fact too easy to lean on him, to cheat him. But he always knew this, and yet did not wish to know it. He saw through all the young men in whose veneration he felt the need for security, knew the reverse side of praise and the sham of camaraderie, but he was resolved never to become bitter with such experience and deliberately saw to it that his confidence was strengthened. I recall one such episode which perfectly sums up this unshakeable trust. I paid a visit to Deman, his publisher and one of his childhood friends, to ask if I could obtain a rare first edition which I lacked for my collection. Deman did not have it but, aware of my interest in Verhaeren and not aware I was so intimate with him, he offered me the proof manuscripts of his latest works, containing innumerable variations, for the sum of two hundred to three hundred francs. I told Verhaeren, who laughed royally: 'Oh, he knows me so well,' he exclaimed, 'he knows that I cannot see the proofs again without making interminable revisions to the poems and now I see why he, the otherwise thrifty fellow, sends me the galley proofs eight or nine times per edition. That gains him a thousand francs in profit and provides excellent business for him.' Now that he knew he laughed, and the next time he good-naturedly corrected the proofs whenever they came.

This gift for friendship was truly wonderful, for it possessed that precious enhancement of selflessness that secretly attaches itself to only the most sagacious of men. He had the passion to extend the friendship beyond himself, to unite individual friends. Nothing made him more content than to see that the people whom he loved understood each other and that, so to speak, new elements fused together. And indeed we, Verhaeren's friends, have remained across all the countries of this ripped-apart Europe a community of love, a community in the midst of nations. With him distrust of people was reviled. He would rather overestimate than be responsible for an injustice to an individual, he listened to everyone, never disregarded an opinion, and no outside force was able to shake his confidence once it had sunk its roots deep. There were always people around him (whom are they not?) hard at work to drive a wedge between him and his great companions, alienating him from Lemonnier, to whom he was devoted lifelong with a childlike and truly touching attachment, or between him and Maeterlinck at the moment when he received the Nobel Prize, trying to engineer a rivalry between them. He listened, remained silent and maintained a bitter defiance of self-conviction. His noble nature resisted every conflict and I still remember that unforgettable hour when he once came to our table in Brussels, like one to whom a great, unexpected happiness had fallen, smiling and good-natured as a boy, telling us that he had reconciled himself with the last of his enemies, who had been bitterly opposed to him for twenty years. By chance he had met him at a club in Brussels, and the old, griping adversary had passed him by with a strange, self-conscious look. 'The thought,' said Verhaeren, 'that a living and valuable man, with whom I had once been a friend in youth, wished to avoid me and to deny me seemed so absurd and childish that I felt ashamed such a feeling could even exist.' He spontaneously approached his opponent and shook his hand. Then, radiant, he returned. Now that no one in the whole wide world was against him, he was permitted to love everyone again, to be of service to all. I have never seen him more cheerful as on that day, when he came back and announced, 'I have no enemies left.'

So was this rich life, this great heart constructed, which had windows on the world, doors for all men, and yet firmly persisted in itself. I'm not sure if I can recount how stubbornly this man remained anchored in his foundations, whether I am equipped to depict the marvellous certitude of his actions and passions. He loved life, he loved his self and he was buoyant in his own being, for just as he did not mistrust the other, he lacked suspicion of himself. What undermines most great poets (but in some, like Dostoyevsky or Hebbel, actually inspires greatness) is the question of conscience, right or wrong, whether this was allowed or not; in him such a question remained silent. He followed his instinct, and through his sense of decency possessed the consciousness of always doing the right thing. If he made a mistake then he quietly admitted it, without regret (even the last error of his life, hatred, he had dismissed in his final testimonies), and it was repugnant to him to torment oneself, to whitewash over something. Once, he cycled along a road that was off-limits. He was stopped and sent before the judge. The judge, who knew him, wanted to do him a favour, suggesting that the defendant had apologized for having overlooked the ban on this roadway. But Verhaeren insisted. He had carried on even though he had clearly seen the warning sign and therefore wished to pay the fine rather than lie. Willingly he paid the ten francs. This little episode was typical of the self-assured certitude, the avoiding of nothing and nobody, and thus his life could be so free of secretiveness because he never knew shame and had nothing to hide. There were wild excesses, debts, follies, misses and seemingly wasted years back in his youth, which the mature man in him no longer understood. But he never complained or apologized. 'Ultimately,' he once told me, 'I want to live my life just as I lived it, I love everything as it was, as it is, and I will always love it.' This affirmation of all things, without inquiry over good or evil, this was his strength and the foundation of his prodigious assurance.

And that assurance was what I most wanted to learn from him all these years, because I witnessed how much freedom there was in that carefree existence, how much strength and energy was saved in that straightforward gaze, without squinting left or right. There were no inhibitions, no wavering, he went directly according to his own will. What anyone thought of him was irrelevant. Even in appearance he did not submit to fashion, he bought his clothes in department stores, wandered the centre of Paris with a labourer's scarf about his neck looking more like some engine-fitter, he installed himself calmly and without nervousness before the waiters in the best restaurants clad in his poor workman's coat. Because that's how he wanted it. He never forced himself on anyone; all the chatter left him indifferent. Even in literary matters he possessed an absolute sovereignty without pride. He did what he could, cared little for the effect. He rejoiced in every joy and thumbed his nose at every stupidity and spite.

From this assuredness and worry-free attitude came that directness which was his deepest secret. I have never seen a person speak more freely to others. Partiality was unknown to him; he treated those above and below him equally. In Caillou he went into the woods where woodcutters around a fire carved puppets from the new wood. He sat down jovially with them, for he was keen on anything to do with crafts, and they chatted to him as an equal, offering him tobacco for his pipe, and in the ensuing conversation there was no sense that he was a 'gentleman' or someone educated. Or he would sit down on a bench and a strange woman would sit beside him and he would chat as if to the pastor or a servant; sometimes people would come to the house and ask him to write a request or a letter to their son (they knew little about him other than that he was a 'scribe'), and he did so without treating it like a joke or a task that was beneath him. The naturalness with which people came to him delighted him more than the greatest success. In the neighbouring village, his friend the draughtsman had received some minor medal and the whole district prepared for the banquet. Good-natured and cheerful, he sat among the citizens and made a speech, he attended christenings and weddings and spoke the same language as the ordinary folk. And the next morning he was invited by King Albert to the Ostend palace; he spoke to the ministers and most influential people of the time about the most important problems, equally at ease with both groups, always easy in his own mind, with his clear view of the essence of the people and therefore always free, always carefree. Never have I seen him insecure in any situation, never was the straight axis of his strength bowed. Even in foreign cities, where he did not know the language, he willed himself on. And out of these thousand small anonymous victories he gained a heightened feeling of life...

The curious, those who did not properly know him, often asked me if he was poor or rich, independent or dependent. No one knew. He lived simply and was always hospitable. He acquitted himself like a modest ordinary citizen and gave money generously. He lived in a small barn over the summer and lifelong refused any commissioned literary work or to take an official position. Freedom in life and an unfettered will was the highest calling for him. He was not attached to any profession or associations, he took no sides in this party or that, he only made spontaneous human decisions, and he was also immune from the last constraint of our time, money. He managed to remain independent without being rich, preferring simplicity rather than the least restriction of freedom. He had lost a part of his father's inheritance early; so what he had at the time of his marriage was nothing more than a modest pension. He preferred to hole up in a couple of rooms as if he were compelled to do so, and even in later years when fame found him he did not allow himself to be lured out of this assuredness. As a young man he still had his passions, collected valuable books, paintings. One day he decided to sell them all, keeping only those of his friends; the word 'possessions' no longer had power over him, for everything he owned was through enthusiasm. He did not care whether a picture he loved was in the Louvre or his own front room, and even this tiny little house in Caillou, which he filled with so much of himself and gave to the world in his poetry, was only ever a rented property. When, finally, the financial harvest came, he did not know what to do with it; for his wishes were satisfied, his existence on the margins freer than in the lap of luxury. Fame and success left no trace on his outward life. Uninhibited by fear, untroubled by anxiety, not plagued by ambition, not tormented by shame and remorse, divinely free and heedless, he lived his rich life in the midst of the petty bourgeois, and from his presence I learnt that true freedom was not in the excitement of indulging desires, but in contentment from a rejection of desire and finding in the very act of freedom the highest fulfilment.

So quietly and free-spirited this life went by, and he loved it and cherished this love. His poetry, could it be anything more than an unremitting utterance of his existence in all its rich detail, an affirmative to the present, to the city, to nature, to the people and to himself? In everything, he saw what lived as being equally worthy of love, and if he affirmed and admired life in all its forms, it was never for their own sake alone, but to be enhanced through them. He was enthusiastic about his own enthusiasm in order to feel more through this ardour of being, and sometimes it was pure intoxication that emanated from him. Always, at any given hour, he was ready to let those flames surge forth. In art galleries before canvases, among new people, in the theatre, in lectures, his being rose up, he suddenly became eloquent, his enthusiasm mounted, he spoke like a preacher, with every nerve strained to the utmost, his breast tense, resounding and broad. Only those who had witnessed him in one of these ecstasies really knew him, and what's more these ecstasies were not fleeting moments, but often grew like forest fires, raging for weeks and months. When he returned from Russia his whole being was intoxicating to be around. He talked for hours and hours, his memory never exhausted, and you could not be beside him at such moments without glowing inwardly yourself. Every exaltation flared up in him. Once, years ago, I came to Brussels from Strasbourg; that morning I had stood before the cathedral, for it was that memorable day when, for the first time, a Zeppelin ventured out on its long-distance journey. I told him how the city was when, suddenly startled by the gun salutes, people stormed into the streets in their thousands, bloomed at the windows, twined around the chimneys and, as if with a single cry, so to speak, rose up into the sky. He glowed with the ardour of it, for every new invention, every bold step of the human spirit and the absence of frontiers between nations. The next day, early in the morning, he came rushing into my room clutching the newspaper in his hand; he had read of the Zeppelin catastrophe of Echterdingen and was desperate, almost close to tears. Already he had imagined man had conquered the air and the shining dream of the new humanity glowed within him. Such a misfortune felt like a sudden defeat. But it was not only the great things that made him enthusiastic: the workings of a clock, a stanza in a poem, a picture, a landscape, anything could enchant him. And since he always yearned to see the positive, the creative in all things, as I have already articulated, life for him was infinitely rich and beautiful because it was inexhaustible. He loved Europe and the world beyond his home, loved the future above the past because it still offered possibilities of the new, unforeseen possibilities of rapture and exaltation, and without any fear of death he could love life endlessly. As the world expanded alongside his own life, he cheered yes and yes!, increasing his rejoicing. In such moments the aged man suddenly became young again and at the same time a prophetic patriarch, his flame lighting up the silent room with a word: you felt in the fiery current as if you were torn open and your own blood entered his rhythm. You felt his doctrine of 'Toute la vie est dans l'essor' as the highest possible exaltation and self-gratification; you could never indulge in the trivial in the hours and days after being in his company. Oh, those hours of ecstasy, of excitation, I have never known better!

Because of this enthusiasm and the burgeoning increase of his strength, his work was a daily requirement. In his work he uncoiled himself, his verses brought casual feeling into the high-flown limbo of the day. It was for him an irrepressible urge to renew his vitality, the fountain of youth of his joy. He did not write in the latter years of his life as the layman would imagine a lyric poet would, out of an occasional need, from an outpouring of emotions, but rather from a constant necessity for self-improvement. For him never a day passed without work. It was essential to him, not as for many others out of avarice or ambition, but as a tonic for the blood, the lever of his mental powers. What others might do in the morning, such as sport or exercise, strengthening the physical being, was for him the work—some process of maintaining the circulation of his spiritual personality, an inflammation of the enthusiastic element. His work, then, was more than just diligence or inspiration: it was already a function of his nature. I recall him saying that when he turned sixty he would no longer care to write anything. By then one is weary, there is no possibility to renew oneself, one merely repeats oneself, one compromises the created work. So a few years went by, then I saw him again in his fifty-eighth year and he declared that he did not wish to write another line after the age of seventy. I could not resist reminding him with a smile that only a short time ago he had spoken of the sixtieth year as the limit of lyric achievement and expressed my happiness that he had gone back on his earlier decision. Verhaeren gazed at me, astonished at first, then smiled softly. 'It's true that after my sixtieth year my verses will be quite worthless, but what can I do about it? You get so used to it, so long a compulsion. What else remains of life? The other enthusiasms have fallen by the wayside: women, curiosity, travels, vitality. The work remains, the desk as the only activity. It may be valueless to others, but for myself, when I get up from the table, I always feel as light as if I have been in flight.' Oh, he was aware of it all, even his flaws and endangerments!

Thus every day began with work. Straight out of sleep he threw himself into the fiery universe of lyrical upsurge. Of course, for a long time his poetry was not pure lyricism, unconsciously crystalline, but a laborious, almost methodical attempt to master the verse form. Just as the farmer, before he ploughs, prepares the field, so inwardly he divided his world into cycles. He worked programmatically, tenaciously, calmly and consciously, his strong will delimiting the circle of his activity in advance. He sometimes worked on several poems at the same time, but they were always cyclical and connected by substance, and as soon as one part of the work was finished, he put it aside. I know that if I state this publicly I will upset for some the notion of Verhaeren as the lyric poet (all those who believe only in the musty idea of the mystical birth of the poem), and I will disappoint them even more if I tell them there was always a rhyming dictionary on his desk and a thesaurus, that even Verhaeren occasionally noted strange words and certain rhyming names in notebooks and on blank sheets to use them later in his poems. In fact, from time to time, he would first consult the map before summoning the vision of the world in a poem. Gradually Verhaeren had become a great technician of the poem more than a spontaneous lyricist, but, more importantly, until the last day his very being was lyrical and passionate, his upsurge tremulous with the rhythm of the blood. He completed his poems coolly but created them as a man inflamed. Not any longer with a burning grip, but just as a rough peasant scores furrow after furrow from the eternal field of the world, so day after day he dug out a few more lines of his cosmic poems. And this work was his passion, his good fortune and his eternal rejuvenation.

His most beloved work within work, however, was perfection. He was passionate about hammering and pounding the verses into shape, and his corrections reveal the relentless force of his will to achieve perfection. His manuscripts resemble battlegrounds where the prone corpses of the fallen words lie crosswise, with new recruits scrambling over them, but all are mown down by the inexorable, and from this tumult finally is forced the new, permanent form. He recast the old verses (not always for the better, I feel) from one edition to the next. With circumspection and piety, his friends sought to prevent him from altering those that had already become personified and unified. But he never gave in as long as a book had not been printed; time and again he plunged headlong into the work, stabbing at syllables and exchanging words, and so intense was his fear of his own fury of revision that he almost never opened his own books when they were completed. When he went on a journey, he carried the large bag with his manuscripts strapped around his body like a Sioux chief, and at night they lay beneath his pillow, so much did he fear for them. But once the embers had died down, for him the work was forgotten. Indeed, numberless were the poems that were lost from his memory. When he rummaged in old magazines or leafed through pale, yellowed manuscripts on grey, rainy days, he was himself astonished to find there his own poems of which he was oblivious, having no idea of when and if he had written them, and his judgement was unbiased, clear, and lacked all egotism, as that of a stranger.

But it was a true celebration when any great poem was completed, when he leant back in the armchair, the freshly written papers in his hand, his pince-nez pressed to his myopic eyes, and began to read aloud in his sonorous, somewhat harsh voice. Gradually all his muscles tensed, his hands rose to the final curl of his mane, the finest hair of his drooping moustache quivering with the rhythm of the verses, and the sentences, the stanzas, rang out ever more metallic in the room. He grasped the sentences, swung them and they vibrated at their ends, clanging more strongly and more powerfully, they spoke until all was rhythm, and he as well as we were filled to overflowing. Like a wave rising and falling, the breath rose and fell, sometimes sprayed like foam over a pointed word, and the storm that emanated from him whipped the broad, flowing verses wildly into each other. His own form, normally diminutive, grew larger in these moments of heightened excitation, and I cannot now read all those poems I first heard read without sensing his voice, which instilled in them their deepest and most veracious life. They were the hours of celebration behind the work, the little festive moments in the quiet of the day, unforgettable to all who experienced them, and shrouded only by the tragic thought that they are irretrievable.

He was not the type to hide himself away, he wandered the city streets and whoever sought him out found him easily enough. There was no mystery about his nature, he was entirely open in the clear light of life, and his traits, which I am trying to reproduce from memory, were familiar to many. But behind it, in the private domain of his life as it were, invisible to most and yet inseparable, like the shadow that first lends a form its depth in space, stood the silent figure of his wife, almost unnoticed and unknown. One cannot speak of his life without remembering it, the steady inner flame, the luminance of his life. Only those who entered the house knew of it, and of these only the most intimate. So modest, so shadow-like, she remained a step behind him. She had never been pictured in the journals, was never seen at society events and in the theatres—even in their home the casual visitor would only notice her at the table or as a fleeting presence passing through the room, like a smile on a serious face. For this noble woman had thus transformed the meaning of her life, that her sole ambition was to immerse herself in this work, in this existence, in order that the poetic strengths of her husband could fully evolve. As a young woman she had been a painter, and one of rare talent, but from the day of her marriage she had shrugged off all public activity. She was now simply a spouse, simply a wife. Here and there in quieter hours she might paint a small picture, a portrait of Verhaeren, a corner of the garden, a view into a room, but never were these biographical pictures entered for a show or seen in public. How hard it was for friends even to get to lay eyes on these works by her, the most modest! Not to her but to Verhaeren one was obliged to appeal if one wanted to gain access to the small barn which served as a studio.

This woman, Marthe Verhaeren, was the last secret in his enviable way of living. Only those who were close to him knew where this wonderful peace and security, this reassurance came from, which embraced him. Only we who knew who the St George of his poem was, who had rescued him from the mire of nerves, the tumult of passions. Only those closest knew what a wise, sober counsellor she was to him in all matters, how much motherliness was mingled with the tenderness of the childless, and how she was prudent never to impinge on the innermost will of his nature, his freedom. People sat talking at the table, in twos and threes, the black coffee was duly served, and suddenly she was gone, without so much as a goodbye. She wanted to leave the men with him in conversation. She knew that whoever had made the pilgrimage to Saint-Cloud or Caillou sought him, the poet, and how superfluous, how lacking in culture most artists' wives can be. She did not even accompany him to the dress rehearsals of his plays, the thought was insupportable to her that politeness might bring her success, and she also happily left him to friends when they were travelling. Her virtue lay beneath the surface, yet was wonderfully beneficial due to the silent non-renunciation, the constant propensity to sacrifice anonymity. Her entire being desired nothing but his joy and gratitude.

And really and truly, here was a reward equal to the labour, for who knew how to thank like Verhaeren? The three books he dedicated to her seem, in spite of the breadth of his oeuvre, perhaps the most imperishable, the most personal of all his poetry. Here, for those who know him, every word is rich with the tone of his voice. The place, the little garden, the room in which dwells the stillness of evening, the whole of life, they are raised up like praying hands, and even in his war book, that distorted cry of grief, the one poem to her shines like a lonely flower in a crater landscape of volcanic meaning, as when outdoors, absorbed in conversation, they watch from the heights of Saint-Cloud as the aeroplanes circle above, and how, tragically and beautifully, their mutual feeling of compassion blends with the shudder of war. So impressively he gave thanks, as long as there was breath remaining in his soul and a word at his lips. Now that his duty has faded away, it is ours, friends, to guard his thanks as a legacy.

Small was the house and small the table. For long years we sat in twos and threes together, and outside the world carried on. Friends came and went, the whole of life it seemed, peoples and times, streamed through that room, came and went. But then a new guest arrived, a new friend, who came more often and, in the end, never left: Fame. Every day now he occupies the house, a busy, well-meaning, an unwelcome and yet not unwelcome guest. Each morning he drops a shock letter on the breakfast table. He bears telegrams and invitations. He brings to the table pictures, coins and banknotes, books and admiring dedications from all countries. He draws in new faces with his tempestuous hand: young poets who want to see the master, the inquisitive, petitioners and reporters. Every day he extends himself, becomes ever more bustling and familiar, until you are constantly aware of his presence. And yet Fame, otherwise so aggravating and dangerous, who might easily strangle the work of the host and position himself in its place, in this house never takes on an insolent and loud bearing. Here there is just too much security, too much strength. Here Fame, great European Fame, can do nothing to disturb the inner peace.

A little puzzled, we looked at him when he came for the first time and pushed his way into the house, around the time of Verhaeren's fiftieth year. It had long since been expected that he would sit at the tables of others, and there was no envy. He was not shown the door in Caillou or Saint-Cloud, but the place of honour was never accorded him. He was never permitted entry into Verhaeren's real life. And never have I felt Verhaeren's inner human greatness more visibly and powerfully that at that last test of his fame. I had been drawn to his work at a time when barely any of the smallest circles knew of him and he was just seen as one of the Decadents and Symbolists. Who really knew anything of his books back then? Of my own first poems, long since rejected, more copies were sold than his own. In Paris he was no one, and when the name Verhaeren was mentioned, people would say: 'Oh, Verlaine!' But in those days I never once heard him complain. It never affected him inwardly that Maeterlinck, who was ten years his junior, had found fame worldwide, that unspeakably industrious lesser talents were hailed as the great figures of the day, while his own effort kept to the shadows. He laboured, completed his work without enquiring, without hope, though he was always conscious of the inner security of his being, of his work. He never took a step towards fame, never joined the review-beggars and obliging flatterers and never so much as dealt a spade blow at the bridge between his inner work and external success. But when fame arrived and dropped into his hands, he accepted it as a gift, took it like everything else in his existence as an exaltation, as a renewal of life. Gradually a certain national pathos awoke in his verses; he no longer spoke from Flanders, one within the country, but as Flanders itself, as the voice of his people, and the great celebratory addresses he gave at the world fair were already animated by the self-consciousness of the super-personal, the resonance of fame. While in the past poetry was merely a personal passion, in his last years it became an apostolate to him; in his lyrics he felt that he must proclaim the message of the times and the glory of his people. Not as a wreath entwined vainly about his head did he bear his fame, nor as something despicable trodden underfoot. He accepted fame as a *cothurnus*, a thick-soled boot which elevated his stature, raised his sights above his time and his voice above the multitude. Never have I witnessed a poet of our time—with the exception of the brotherly form of Romain Rolland—wear his world renown more beautifully and more responsibly than Emile Verhaeren.

But the curious and infinitely human experience for me, friendly and close to him, was to observe this fame growing year by year, month by month. Living and experiencing it with him, I passed through all its phases, the first rustlings in the dark, the invisible mass of indifference and then, like one word, so to speak, sweeping over the other and suddenly one day the avalanche plunges, whooshing wonderfully yet perilous at the same moment. I have daily witnessed great world fame, clothed in men and letters, disguised as seduction and enticement, fame in all its masks of vanity and danger; today I know everything about it, having experienced it myself. And because I too have experienced it, day after day, and have, without desiring it, attained it myself, I know that I would wear it as strongly and worthily as this exemplary man and, like Verhaeren, live free from this last and most deadly enemy of art and the authentic life.

Memories of that time, of good and great times, scarcely have I called them and already they are in their hundreds, days and hours, episodes and words, endless stormy swarms before the glance of remembering! How they come apart, how they stratify, remove futility from the abundance of happy experience, conversations too carefree and joyful, too blissfully witnessed—how I struggled to hold them faithfully in my own words, individual hours of mutual confidentiality! From all of you now drifts a sweet smoke of melancholy, a dark, swaying sense of gratitude, formless and trickling away like memory-distant summer nights. I sense you as a whole, however much I sense the individual, as the blessed apprenticeship of the heart, as the first realization of human mastery.

Memories, memories, you mighty flood, how to dam you! Where are you, cities we wandered together? Liège, today a fortress stormed and then a city at peace, when we travelled up the river with Albert Mockel and friends on that bright summer's day to visit the most marvellous of all saints, Saint Antoine le Guérisseur. Oh, the laughter and reverence, the conversation in the little hermitage, feeling healthy in the midst of those pilgrims of the sick. In Valenciennes, where we stood before the museum, Brussels with friends, at the theatre, on the streets, in the cafés, in the libraries, Berlin and the hour with Reinhardt, the quiet conversation that afternoon with Eduard Stucken, an oasis of silence in Berlin. Vienna, where in those days not a single poet came to see him, and we were happy enough alone to explore the city like a strange city anew, Hamburg, the journey on the little steamer through the harbour and then out in Blankenese with Dehmel, whose open nature and whose eyes, those of a 'clever shepherd', he so fraternally loved.

Overnight in Dresden and Munich, autumn in Salzburg, Leipzig for Kippenberg with Van der Velde, the old comrade, days in Ostend, evenings by the sea. Oh you countless journeys in conversation, in the Pullman, on our wanderings, how you cajole me, you things of the past! I do not need your urging for love, not your admonition for memory.

And Paris! The modest dinners for three or four, the hours spent in my room, hours with Rilke, Rolland and Bazalgette, where I had the finest people in my life with me at the same moment around a table. That afternoon with Rodin among the stones and the figures, and he himself already stone-like in his fame. The walk through the Louvre, through the museums, the many colourful and always cheerful hours, and then a mournful interlude, that afternoon in the Balkan war, how the news-sellers yelped, Scutari had fallen and we sat and talked, fearful whether today or tomorrow the madness of a world war would spring up before us. And then the prophetic hour, when we stood outside and saw the aeroplanes circling and his voice rose in ecstasy, extolling the accomplishment of humanity, and then fell back in horror, for if this beautiful force were to end in destruction, the mania of the military powers would surely have to be behind it. Oh, the figures and people in the tranquil Saint-Cloud house, in my little Paris room, how often you dwell within me, enveloped now with the consciousness of being lost.

Then again in Caillou-qui-Bique, the lovely paths into the countryside, the civil exchanges with the pastor, the lawyer, the neighbour, friends from near and far. Hours of serenity, of bright episodes of mischievousness when a little provincial lawyer lectured Verhaeren on poetry and how to mend his ways, and Verhaeren listened patiently and earnestly, winking at us and not permitting us to burst into raucous laughter. Or as he read his 'Helena' and conjured the name of the queen and suddenly the door opened and the little Walloon maid was stood there, claiming to hear her own name called as she worked in the kitchen, until she realized from the general merriment that she had confused the name of the queen with her own, and hurried forth into the realm of shadows.

How quickly they passed, these days, and how strong their flow remains unchanged in my heart. Oh, how much more I could recount, for the details are unforgettable, and sometimes in the dream itself the images within me sparkle and possess a curious precious radiance, as if seen through tears.

Just one hour I wish to select from the sparkling roundelay, just one with all its beauty of melancholy. Again I'm in Caillou, it's summer, afternoon. The sun is shining strongly on the red roof, the roses are already drooping wearily, the lilacs hang heavy, soon it will be autumn. I am sitting in the little *bosquet* in front of the house, a colourful tangle of ivy winds in blue shadows. I have just translated a few verses of a poem, then read a little, now I sit there and watch the golden bees swarming about the last blooms. Then, a heavy tread: Verhaeren approaches me, puts his hand on my shoulder. 'Je veux faire une petite promenade avec ma femme, il fait si beau.'

I remain. I know how he likes to go alone in the afternoon, and anyway, it's so pleasant to sit here in the shade and observe the ripening fields. Now he leaves the house, I watch him, his wife on his arm, his hat in his free hand, step out through the little gate into the meadow, which already breathes early autumn. How can he walk so slowly, how can he be so stooped? The body leans forward, the grey hair, once so flaming, the coat carefully placed around the woman's shoulders on such a hot day. Slowly he walks, deliberately and heavy. Gone is the walk of his past, upright and strong, and for the first time I sense: he walks now into old age. Madame Verhaeren also helps him along; she seems tired today too; with short steps they go, pensive, like grandparents, like old peasants on their way to church. I realize, now comes old age, and how beautiful for them it will be, how well they will wear it. They will be Philemon and Baucis, kind and peaceable, away from life, even more ripened and better off than they ever were up to now. The day is warm, the sun shines brightly, but yet, as they go, I feel the magnificence of autumn over the land. Now he raises his hands into the sun, then holds them over his eyes and gazes out for a long time into the unknown. Then they move on together quietly, so quietly, and I watch them for an age, until their forms disappear into the forest, as in a distant time.

I wished to recollect this hour and those others that I did not feel enough for at the time and whose fearful meaning I understood only later. It was in March 1914, in the early spring of that terrible year. Unknowing we were, as all the rest of the world. I'm sitting in my room in Paris, it's morning, I am writing letters to my friends at home. Suddenly I hear footsteps on the stairs, the heavy, deliberate footfall of Verhaeren, whom I know so well and joyfully greet. I jump up and it really is him: he passed by only briefly to inform me that he was travelling to Rouen. A young Belgian composer had set one of his poems in a melodrama and implored him to attend the première. The benevolent human being he was, he could never deny anything to young artists. He was set to depart tomorrow and he had come to ask if I knew Rouen and whether I wished to accompany him. Because he loved to travel with friends, only reluctantly did he travel alone, and I might say in all modesty that he liked to travel with me. It was a pleasure for me and I gladly agreed. In a moment my suitcase was packed and the next morning we met at Gare Saint-Lazare.

Curious: when we travelled by train from Paris to Rouen, the whole four hours we spoke of nothing but Germany and France. He had never revealed himself to me as he did then, never more openly had he related his feelings on Germany. He would always love that great German strength, the German ideal, but what he despised and distrusted was the German government, the caste system of the aristocracy. For him, to whom personal freedom held nothing less than the meaning of life, a people that surrendered it could never be truly alive, and drawing upon Russia by way of comparison, he told me that he found every man in Russia free amidst the general servitude, whereas in Germany, where there is greater freedom, the individual feels within himself too much obedience to the state. At that moment, in this penultimate conversation, we summarized all that we had formerly discussed in a hundred separate conversations and I recall every word precisely because it remains irrevocable. Astonished at how time had flown by, I suddenly noticed we were in Rouen. We wandered the streets and as night fell stood before the cathedral, whose scrollwork shimmered in the moonlight like white lace. How strange this evening! After the conviviality of the little gathering we repaired to a tiny café on the riverside, a handful of sleepy people sat there, but suddenly an old man got up, went over to Verhaeren and greeted him. He was a loose-living friend from his childhood, a minor painter, of whom Verhaeren had heard nothing for thirty years, and yet he embraced him like a brother. The ensuing conversation was enlivened by his youth.

The next day we travelled back. We had only small suitcases and carried them by hand to the station. And as if the blackness of oblivion were rent with a knife, so clearly in the darkness of memory I see the station, the small one high above the city, see the bare tracks before the tunnel, the roaring train, my hand reaching out to help him enter the carriage. And I realize: this is the very place, the place of tragedy, where two years later death sprang on him, and I know the rails and machines whose praise he sang tore him apart like the Maenads' Orpheus, their singer.

This was in the spring, the spring of 1914. The terrible year had begun. Silently and peacefully it grew and slowly matured into summer. According to our arrangement, I was intending to stay with Verhaeren in August, but had come to Belgium earlier to spend three weeks at the coast. En route I stopped off for a day in Brussels, and my first priority was to visit Verhaeren at the home of his friend Montald. A little tramway goes out there, down a broad avenue at first and then through fields to the village of Woluwe, and there I found him with his friend, who was just finishing off a new portrait of him, the final one. How good it was to see him there. We talked of his work, the new collection *Les Flammes hautes*, from which he read the last poems to me, and excerpts from his play *Les Aubes*, which he revised for Reinhardt. We spoke of friends and the summer months, when we hoped to share much happiness together. We sat there for three or four hours, the garden shone bright and verdurous, the sheaves swayed in the wind and the world breathed peace and the scent of fruits. Our parting was brief, because we would be seeing each other again soon in that tranquil house in Caillou, and once again he hugged me and we bid our farewells. I was to arrive on 2nd August, and he called out to me again, '2nd August!'. We were so light of heart we thought nothing of the date. The tram bore me back through summer fields. For a long time, I saw him standing alongside Montald, waving until he vanished for ever.

I still had some quiet days before me at Le Coq. But then the storm clouds gathered over the homeland. Each day I went into Ostend to survey the papers, and the certainty drew closer. Then came the ultimatum: now it sunk in and I relocated to Ostend so as to be prepared. We were all still brothers together, my Belgian friends Ramah and Crommelynck, we went to visit James Ensor (whom half a year later German soldiers wanted to shoot as a spy), but the joy of the world melted away in those terrible July days. As the month drew to a close, we were still sitting together in a café, still with the old spirit of mutual trust. The drumming went on, soldiers passed: Belgium mobilized. It seemed incomprehensible to me that Belgium, the most peaceful country in Europe, was organizing itself into a state of readiness, and there I was still joking about the machine guns hauled by dogs, making light of the little troops of Belgian soldiers passing with their severe expressions. But my Belgian friends were not laughing. They were anxious. 'On ne sait pas, on dit que les Allemands veulent forcer le passage.' At this I just laughed. It seemed preposterous, the idea that the Germans, thousands of whom were bathing and lounging on the beach just over there, would invade Belgium by force of arms! And with deep conviction I reassured them, saying: 'You can hang me from this lamp post if Germany ever marches into Belgium.'

But the news became ever more ominous. Austria had already declared war. I saw that my situation was almost untenable. I wrote a line to Verhaeren, informing him of my intention to travel home, and I arrived just in time to secure a seat on the packed train. What a journey! People troubled, silent, concerned, anxiety in eyes shining with fever, one exciting another in violent conversations; and the express train which could not go fast enough. At every moment we leapt to the door to check the stations. At last, Brussels! We grabbed at newspapers all carrying contradictory accounts. Then came Liège, which seemed as yet unsuspecting, then Verviers, the border station. It was only when the wheels began to turn, slowly moving the coaches from Belgian to German territory, that an indescribable sense of relief on finally finding sanctuary enveloped us. But immediately, in open country, the train stopped dead, five minutes passed, ten minutes, a quarter of an hour, a half-hour. We had left Belgium and were in German territory, a stone's throw from Herbestal, and yet we could not enter the station. We waited and waited. Anguish came over me, an anguish which had no real sense, a mortal terror had suddenly gripped me, a terror that I dared not explain. The dull thunder of trains continued ominously into the night, the wagons heavily loaded, their cargo hidden beneath canvas, so you couldn't make out what was there. But someone at my side whispered 'Guns!' For the first time we came face to face with the war. I recalled the anxiety of my Belgian friends, their thought filled with horror and disgust: Germany really was threatening Belgium with arms. Finally, that interminable half-hour passed and slowly the train entered the station. I dashed onto the platform to buy a newspaper. Not one could be found. I wanted to enter the waiting room, to force a way in. Strange! Entry was forbidden. A guard with a white beard barred the way, St Peter guarding the door to heaven. There was a genuinely grave mystery in his dignity. From within issued the sound of voices and the rattle of weapons. I knew now that I had no need to open a newspaper the next day to learn anything more: I had seen the horror unfold. Germany was invading Belgium: war, European war, which nothing could stop. The locomotive whistled. I rejoined my carriage and the train continued on, into the very heart of the country. On 1st August, it was war.

The fiery curtain had fallen between us. There were no bridges between countries. What once formed an amicable connection in nerves and thoughts now was obliged to call itself an enemy. (Never, not even for one hour have I been able to do it!) The familiar voices from abroad no longer reached each other, nothing was known about the other in those first months of the apocalyptic year, all voices were shattered in the roar of the collapsing world. At last I heard his, Verhaeren's, voice through the smoke and I barely recognized that voice any more, so foreign had it become, so shrill in its hatred, that voice which was once filled with goodness and purity of passion.

At that time I was silent, publicly kept my silence. For him the route to me was blocked, but I did not speak to those in Germany who out of a misunderstood sense of duty heaped great insults on his entire existing oeuvre and mind. There were those who urged me to bear witness and provide a testimony, but I have learnt to stay silent in a world of the oppressed and wounded. Never will anyone succeed in having me play the judge or prosecutor over one who was a master to me and whose pain I had to venerate as just and sincere even in his wildest and most repugnant outburst. I knew that he whose homeland had been destroyed at Antwerp, whose country seat of Caillou was occupied by German soldiers, that he, the exile of his country, would find his way back to the world; I knew that he was strong enough to conquer himself again. I knew that hatred in this man, whose supreme objective was reconciliation, could not be permanent, and already in the second year I encountered the old voice again in the moving introduction to his book of hatred [*La Belgique sanglante*, 1915]. Already I felt that much closer to him and again a year later, in 1916, when I published an essay on a European theme, 'The Tower of Babel',* in *Carmel*, a Swiss monthly magazine, where I called for the unity of spirit as the highest affirmation the hour demanded, I suddenly received through a mutual Swiss acquaintance a message containing his heartfelt approval. I confess it was a joyful day for me when I received that message, for I knew that the veil which clouded his vision was torn and I knew how irreplaceable he would be for us in the coming times, passionate in his greatness and unifying power, as he had been terrible in his hatred and wrath.

But how differently it all turned out, how differently! A friend bursts into my room, the still-damp newspaper in his hand, and points with his finger to a telegram stating that Verhaeren is dead, torn apart by machines. As much as I was accustomed to the lies propagated in newspapers during the

---

* Included in *Messages from a Lost World*, Pushkin Press, 2017.

war, the untruth and the rumours, I realized this message was fact and unalterable right from the first. What died there was something distant and unattainable, one to whom I was not even permitted to send a message, whose hands I was forbidden to clasp by a law, whom to love was still seen by others as an outrage and a crime.

But, in the same moment, I felt the urge to strike my fist against the invisible wall of absurdity that divided us, and which wrenched me away from following him on his final path. There was no one to whom I could express what I felt. For pain and grief, were they not considered a crime in such times? It was a dark day.

A dark day I still remember and will never forget. I took out the letters, the countless letters, to read them again and just be alone with them, to close what was now closed, for I knew: now he would not come. And yet, I could not do it; something within refused to bid farewell to one who lives in me as the blood incarnate example of my existence, of my first belief. And the more I told myself he was dead, the more I felt how much of him still breathes and lives in me, and the very words that I write to say goodbye to him for ever have for me returned him to life. For only the knowledge of immense loss reveals the ephemeral nature of true possession. And only the unforgettable dead are so surely alive!

ARTHUR SCHNITZLER ON HIS SIXTIETH BIRTHDAY

(1922)

R AISED IN HIS CITY, his world, I have loved Arthur Schnitzler the poet at a distance since the first dawn of consciousness, and I love him still more, for those many occasions I have witnessed the marvellous, warm, benevolent fullness of his humanity whose purity is proven. It would be easy for me to laud him with praise on this, his festive day. But the occasion demands that I go further: I wish to speak with that sincerity we have come to know from Arthur Schnitzler himself, what we learnt of him across the whole range of human affairs, and to openly declare with equal sincerity that my faith in his work exceeds that of the present hour (no matter how vociferous its demonstrations may be).

For I feel in truth, in the innermost, sincerest truth, that Arthur Schnitzler's work now, at the hour of his sixtieth birthday, is undergoing a serious, probably the most serious, crisis in terms of its internal and external effect on an audience. That fundamental part of his oeuvre, that of his theatre, of his novels, that narrative of morality, is not afforded the sympathy and recognition it deserves, most notably by today's younger generation: they, the young, are unlikely to grasp the importance of works that seem so enchanting to our eyes, and in some way I can understand why the oncoming generation (and it alone) are left nonplussed by works of art whose intellectual appeal, whose poetic intention they undoubtedly fail to understand. They sense some connection has been broken, and we know what has caused the rupture: the time, the war, that unprecedented transformation of the whole creative sphere which has turned Austria into the most bitter state. A similar thing happened to Stifter in Austria around 1866 and Jean Paul in Germany around 1870: suddenly a youth emerged, liberal there, busily active here, which, following a war, no longer found itself and its problems reflected in such ethereal, finely wrought forms. Once more the tide of history had to turn and swing backwards until we recognized and properly felt these poets again. But time had turned away from them only gradually: in contrast, the world of Arthur Schnitzler was scythed down in a hurricane of only five short years with a violence unknown to history, so a poet like him experienced something unparalleled, his world out of which he created an entire culture over such a lengthy period seemed obliterated. The types, the unforgettable characters that he created yesterday, that on his fiftieth birthday could be observed on the street, in the theatres, in the drawing rooms of Vienna, almost copied as it were from his gaze, have abruptly vanished from the real world, totally transformed. The 'sweet girl' prostitutes herself, the Anatols are playing the stock markets, the aristocrats have fled, the officers are now clerks and agents—the light tone of conversation has coarsened, eroticism has become popularized and the city itself has become the playground of the masses. Furthermore, some of the problems that he treated with such spiritual deftness and poignancy have assumed new levels of intensity, namely the Jewish question and social problems. Conflict without equal: across his oeuvre it was like a mirror held up before the Austrian world, this admirable depiction of the Viennese and Austrian spirit. Then old Vienna succumbs overnight and the new one, which so hastily sought to find itself in such a received image, was summarily unable to recognize itself. It is not he who has betrayed his world, but rather it is reality which has betrayed the poet.

No artist is spared such a crisis. Some experience it at the beginning of their work, or then, when the epoch they have foretold does not recognize itself, and others when their world gradually begins to fade away. But Schnitzler's world—an unprecedented fate—has been wrenched from his hands before it has even faded, before it lived its life. And it would have gone before, had not a man like Arthur Schnitzler nailed it down, preserved it, if it had not lived on in those forms and types, in its spirit and feeling, in the indestructible presence of art in those character portraits, the immutable design that was his work. It is only by appearance that an artist exists through his epoch, a poet through his temporal sphere: in truth, the epoch exists only because of him. It is not the epoch that lasts while the work fades away: the epoch ages, but the work is renewed as a culture, a costume, eternal past in the present. All that was Vienna at the turn of the century, this Austria on the eve of collapse, will one day be rightly recognized only through Arthur Schnitzler, and—for the Franz-Joseph dynasty's name spans too much time—rightly named only after him. It was not the poets who articulated the early years of our Austrian culture: Haydn, Schubert, Waldmüller speak solely for the beginning of the century. Then Grillparzer, Stifter, Raimund emerge as sculptors, as interpreters of this city, this empire. After them there might have been silence, or only music again: yet here he stands at the end of the century, spirit of this city's spirit, true to its traditions and conjuring out of light and reflective games, in diaphanous yet enduring forms, the essence of this remarkable culture. Only a few more years, a decade perhaps, then time will leave its soft patina to darken his images and figures. What today seems the present of yesterday, then becomes purely past, taking on classical form, accessing poetic eternity, and a young generation, a second or third, will partake in our love, endorse our reverence for this serious artist lurking behind such frivolity and lightness. May he encounter that generation enjoying the full measure of his creative strength!

FRANS MASEREEL

Man and Creator

(1923)

A S FORTUNE WOULD HAVE IT, I happen to know with
certainty that Frans Masereel, the most masterly of all
modern artists in the medium of the woodcut, was born on
30th June 1889 in Blankenberge to happily married, middle-
class parents; otherwise I might have presumed he was the son
of Walt Whitman, one of those missing extramarital offspring
whom the American world man conceived during his stay in
the south with an unknown mother. For never have I encountered in one person, in a contemporary artist so much of the
Whitman type of free and yet self-controlled, burly yet serene
force, this irresistible receptivity to all life's appearances, and a
similarly precise natural equilibrium between personality and
environment. In truth, only in the rhythms of Walt Whitman
and that cataract of adjectives, that shattering force of the
ever-burgeoning Whitmanian enumeration, could one describe
his appearance: lofty, virile, muscular, attentive, yet gentle,
at once dark-eyed and bright-eyed, powerful at the point of
utmost gentleness, dynamic in benevolent goodness, cheerful
in workaday earnestness, unrestrained, truly free and solitary
in the inner voice, listening with supreme clairaudience to the
full orchestra of his world. His open, frank demeanour lends
his art, his life the overarching expression of independence.
One can never think of him as self-conscious, neither in the
sense of insecurity nor of shame, for in his presence one enjoys

the rarest of all human spectacles: the authentically free being, inwardly dedicated, yet devoted to all. One must reckon the sum of his inner strengths in order sufficiently to admire him, not just through the already monumental oeuvre, but through the primeval, elemental qualities of his nature.

He is one of our most powerful masters, the archetypal man of the time; however, nothing in his nature, in his work suggests the demoniacal genius. But let's not forget: there exists one (very high, perhaps the highest) type of artist, in whom genius arises from a confluence of powerful forces. I do not think that Handel, Rubens, Whitman, Tolstoy, Balzac (in spite of the bust by Rodin) have during their lives produced any impression other than that of a relentlessly evolving natural force. It is given to such consummate individuals to labour on a daily basis, creating out of an undying restlessness, as if in a perpetual stream. It is not for them to suffer the creative blocks and mental stagnations, the psychic shoals and sudden pre-cipitousness of the intellectual neurotic, but rather experience a harmonious productivity, perennially welling like a spring, which creates power out of their own life force, and only from such a naturally germinated 'non-effort' can such a striking abundance emerge, a rich diversity of world, as Handel with his music, Rubens with his pictures, Whitman in his verses, as this today still-young, unspent man has created in perhaps a thousand woodcuts. In such natures, the productive element appears to relinquish the sudden, the miraculous, because it merely represents organic function, whilst the true miracle occurs in the breadth and reach of the work as a whole, in its unfathomable abundance, its incalculable horizon.

Such natures, and perhaps only they alone, have the true gift of universality. Only those who are open to everything, closed to nothing, who have no predilection for their love of the world, perceive that world and each of its forms as objects, and the entire register of light and dark keys lies poised beneath their hand. A Handel can create serene operas and artful arias such as the tragic *Messiah* and the fortunes of the prophets, a Whitman sings in the same breath of the body of a woman and skyscrapers on Broadway, then we have Balzac illustrating the fate of an ageing provincial maid like the Battle of Beresina and the stock-market affairs of a perfumery dealer: only they who have the necessary equanimity of forces, those who are patient and lack any one mood-dominating root, those with uninhibited productivity, only they can give an *orbis pictus*, both the cosmopolitan and the cosmic image. My feeling is that Masereel, in possessing this organic fullness, advances ahead of all other living draughtsmen and illustrators. For him the whole world in all its objects, appearances and forms represents an equally valid motive for the creation of his drawings and woodcuts; even today the tireless one has produced such a quantity that, like the pictorial writing of the Egyptians, the whole external world, our world, can there be deciphered. Even if all else were to perish, all books, monuments, photographs and documents, and if only the woodcuts he left us over the last ten years were all that remained, they would be sufficient to reconstruct the full measure of our current world, revealing how we lived and how we dressed. There would be communicated the full horror of the war, no holds barred, with all its maleficent machines and grotesque forms, stock exchanges and factories, train stations and ships and towers and fashions and people, yes, all the different types, and furthermore the whole menacing spirit and genius, the mental tempo of our age, for surely in his woodcuts are they best understood. Which artist merits our praise, other than he, the Benjamin of the graphic, for such a quantitative and documentary achievement (for now I shall leave the qualitative aside)? Who of them, in terms of multiplicity and diversity, has done anything even comparable among his contemporaries? Diligence alone could not accomplish this, and technique no less; a higher force was required, a conjoining of elements, something all-encompassing, that marvellous openness of being for the sum total of all phenomena and at the same time a fanatical passion for detail. Masereel is the opposite of an explosive, wildly leaping nature; his spirit, his nature reminds of Balzac, or a Whitman who focuses purely on the universal. He embraces all nations on an equal footing, all languages, all epochs, the old and the new, the romantic and the mechanical, and I know of no animosity that this passionate friend of the world feels towards humanity on our earth, unlike the counter-element, those state institutions whose whole meaning and intention is to reduce the tremendously vital, blood-driven fullness of existence to a state of cooling, to stagnation, to conformity, seeking to constrict and redefine genuinely lived life. Masereel is thus an enemy of the state, whenever it promulgates violence and injustice, an enemy of the 'society' that sees itself as a presiding entity seeking to retain its power at any cost; and without being a politician (he abhors all parties as restrictive forces, placing rigid limits on inner freedom) he has always fought side by side with the weak, the oppressed and the disadvantaged. In his wordless picture-novels *25 Images of a Man's Passion*, *The Idea* and *The Sun*, in his imaginary autobiography, he laid bare all the drives and impulses around the freedom of the individual faced with hostile powers, employing grotesque caricatures he paraded the warmongers, speculators, judges, police, all the

representatives of a selfish morality, a selfish motive. His idea
of the world tolerates nothing that violates the world, any single
group that stymies the sacred unity of the universe. His genius
is always targeted at the whole: like Whitman, who seeks to
distil the world into a thousand stanzas, he wants to distil the
world into images, to portray them in boundless complexity
through thousands of details, without ever compromising that
sense of unity.

He has created tens of thousands of drawings and woodcuts
up to the present time, and despite his unrivalled productivity he
has no reason to fear that he may never finish, for his visionary
capacity is as boundless as the world itself. Like Balzac, Masereel
has a keen eye for the image. Whatever has struck him only the
once, just in passing, or even as reproduction, is fixed in clear,
unfaltering lines within his inner being; behind his forehead lies
a huge compendium of all earthly external forms. He knows
by heart all he has ever seen, even in the most fleeting form.
He never employs a model, nor does he make a preparatory
study for a drawing, never does he consult a costume catalogue
in order to reproduce something, to render a motif 'correctly'.
His memory is as infallible as his hand; he knows (and this truly
has a bearing in some distinctly magical way on all who know
him) each element of the world by heart and breathes life into it
with each detail and at each moment. He knows every spar on
a sailboat, every piston on a locomotive, each stitch he makes
from his network of memory. He might recollect the turban on
a pilgrim to Mecca, the tattoo of a redskin warrior, the parade
march and rifle butt of a Prussian fusilier. He captures every
movement; the shortening of the body in flight, the curvature
of a moving train, the rearing horse, the leaping fish, laughter
and pain wrought on an earthly face. I have often observed

this marvellous man with a sense of wonderment: walking with him in a foreign city, enrapt in the most intense conversation. He seems completely absorbed, lost. And yet a year later you notice in a woodcut a doorknocker from that same street down which you strolled, with all its details meticulously reproduced as if he had secretly photographed it, or the face of a dog which had leapt across his path: that dark eye behind the round, horn-rimmed spectacles can seize a living thing just by a brief encounter with it, and the image is simply drawn inwards like an exposed plate, ready to be archived in the vast storehouse of his memory, where nothing corrupts and decays, but rather everything drifts wave-like, an infinite cosmos of detached forms, until a sign from the will calls for individual lines and has them flow out magically into his hand.

This unprecedented memory of the million moving forms of life and the unremitting willingness with which each of these forms finds the draughtsman's hand, the working knife, is what lies behind Masereel's true genius. Not in the detail, not in a salient, characteristic trait, but in the fullness of abilities, in the scope of visions, here is where the demon genius of the work lies. And, mysteriously, it fuses within him to another seemingly bourgeois virtue, namely his industrious, patient doggedness. I have already stated that something outwardly un-demonic is also present in his nature, a certain heaviness, a gentle, almost rural slowness, recalling the tenacious, steady tread of the farmer trudging across a field at sowing or harvest time, express-ing himself in an artistic sense, this mindfulness of progress towards an infinite goal through some brazen, granite assiduity, a fanatical objectivity found in that *Nulla sine linea* of the old German masters. Each day Masereel is sat in front of his table with his knife for hours on end like a goldsmith, an engraver, a watchmaker, like all great men with their healthy, virtuous crafts, and like them he loves his craft, wherein something of the medieval, the primitive resides. Today he works in the city of Paris, bathed in electric light and carved up with subways, through which a thousand magnetic currents flow, labouring like some mythical ancestor before him who might have forged the old woodcuts of Torhout, those pious image sheets, in the same tiny room, with the same simple technique, with the same knife burrowing into the same wood, with the same indomitable and steady patience. And he loves this technique for the sake of a manly freedom from any model, any prop. All the chemical factories which produce colours could stand silent, the whirring looms weaving cloth from fine threads could fall to bits and he would calmly continue his work. For he requires only a knife and a square block of wood to shape the world, and not even that, for I recall once in Geneva he felled a pear tree himself, hacked it down with an axe and sawed up the wood. If he were cast like Robinson Crusoe on a desert island, after a few days he would be able to work comfortably there, just as well as in his studio, he would form his blocks (I say blocks, because there is something of the sculptor in his mysterious strivings) and make everything come alive in them yet again. He has no need of a particular *ambiance*, no need of assistance, no model, no motive: decades could pass without him even so much as lifting his head from his work, so fulfilled is he inwardly, so restless is his patience. And yet already he has created thousands upon thousands of shapes and forms: I often quipped that now he could easily build a house or a sailing ship out of the same wood which he creatively blended into images and events.

To my mind it is this twofold nature that represents the peculiar charm of Masereel's art, namely that it is so old-fashioned and primal in its artisan technique, as in the days of the block book and family Bibles, and yet its content, its overall impression, its tempo and rhythm are so spectacularly modern and contemporary. He himself once portrayed this twofold nature in a picture that adorns the opening of his book *Memories of My Homeland*. There he stands in self-portrait centred between two worlds, between the two Flanders, between the sensuous, vital dimension of today with his workers, machines and sprawling cities and that of the past, the pious, bell-chiming aura of the churches and monasteries, where with lowered gaze a nun dreams of eternity. He stands irrevocably at the crossroads between flesh and spirit, between primordial strength and the most heightened sense of life. For on the same tiny plates, with the same technique, in that same eight-centimetre space where the old masters forged their saintly legends in rigidly framed, scarcely loosened form, a new element flares up in him: the cinema image. His drawings possess the speed, the pulsating, leaping power of cinematic images (which he endlessly draws forth; he even wrote a film himself), and if you assemble them they display the fast pace of a movie and are equally suspenseful and thrilling. And across each of these plates, with their simple, binary, black-and-white swirls of fiery, nervous rhythm, passes our breathless twentieth century. For him, the most powerful incentive is, through the most severe, colourless form, the woodcut, to compress the most fathomless abundance into the narrowest of spaces, to condense the motion of the event into the smallest reflection across just a few centimetres. That is why these woodcuts are so relentlessly crammed with a thousand details, symbols and simultaneities. At first glance one sees only the most obvious; over time we discern through gradual discoveries the most intriguing paraphrases and contrasts of motif. The longer you gaze into them, the more you discover there. I myself have known them for almost twenty years and never tire of opening the books and portfolios, always finding something new that I had previously overlooked.

But despite this abundance, his work does not remain a mere juxtaposition of things and things, of forms and forms; Masereel is no longer merely an illustrator of books: he began only as a servant of foreign art. Now he has begun to liberate himself to create and write freely, at first with a finite series, like Dürer, Goya and Callot. In recent years Masereel has outgrown the reproductive and created a new graphic-poetic genre: novels, novellas, brief narratives in images without words; and now things have to be quite the other way round for poets to provide the text for these wordless books of a master. I might think of Charles-Louis Philippe or Zola, who translated Masereel's *Passion of a Man* into masterly prose, or Christian Morgenstern, who furnishes the whimsical adventures of his *Book of Hours* with such sublime verses; but as for his favourite book, *The Idea*, I can think of no contemporary poet who could adequately translate this novel into words. For every one of our artist-poets would offer something too artificial, too literal: that is the wonder of Masereel's art, that in all its novelty it is so eminently democratic that it really does create 'good pictures' in the sense that Tolstoy wrote 'good books', so that everyone can understand them, the servant maid, the artist, the student and the professor. And indeed, Masereel's drawings, like Walt Whitman's verses, belong to an imaginary democracy. They are clear to everyone. I would dare to pass them under the noses of workers and photographic apprentices with little in the way of explanation, but on the other hand the greatest artists admire the veracious Expressionism inherent in his works.

Because he senses the world as a whole, he returns again and again to that whole; because he himself belongs to no class in intellectual terms he is able to work competently in terms of both the nation and the people.

This will for worldliness grows irresistibly through his work alongside the art itself. Year after year it was believed that none could measure the widest circle he had reached, for again and again he circles the sphere of reality in an ever-broader, clearer serpentine. If his earlier books were prodigious, his last, *The City*, is truly monumental, infinite, laying bare the modern metropolis with its rich layers of fate, its human masses and all the tragic contrasts between poverty and luxury, debauchery and privation, the pandemonium of its passions. With this work, the artist in him is, one might propose, evolving from sonata form to the symphony.

But as the graphic effort increases, opening up ever-wider horizons through the intensifying power of light, Masereel the artist has at the same time conquered new elements of representation, for after the mighty form now comes colour. His path in this respect was slow, for frivolity is utterly alien to this grounded, steady individual. But step by step he hesitantly moved closer to painting, as though by a circuitous route. At the outset he only managed illustrated drawings, with coloured pencil and tentative theatrical costumes, then came watercolours in which the outline and the graphic gesture still dominated; it was only recently that he began properly to create in colour, and each year sees a more earnest approach to its mysteries. It was as if he had to forcibly wrest, so to speak, from out of the gloom, from the great world-night, the blissful pleasure of the eye, the pleasure in colour, and his first images still carry with them the darkness, the gravity of matter. But from canvas to canvas, from opus to opus, the light of colour becomes more ardent and glowing, it overflows the dividing segregated forms; and now this same irresistibly persuasive power issues from them as from the pages of the graphic works. There is little in the new art of our time to compare to their virility and strength, that robust, almost brutal sensuality: who can easily forget them, these streets of Paris, scenes at the harbour, which appears like a forest, like a monstrous, artificial piece of nature, his fishermen with the heaviness of their bodies, the restrained force held in their outward strength, the women in the cabarets caught in the ghastly illumination of their vice? His graphic opus also represents such a titanic mass of performance, but perhaps it too was just another stage from which his form will now rise to a new, higher outlook onto unequivocal existence.

This, then, in my view is the incomparable power emanating from Masereel. World power, abundance and infinite life, sustained by a pure and strong masculinity. Through its leaves blows the real wind of the world and one feels as if on the bowsprit of a ship, the air from distant climes billowing, the forward force and the tonic, revivifying effect as it emerges from wind and wave, those freest elements. Masereel is as refreshing as anything in the natural world, an ever-intensifying artist, a real bestower of gifts, an invigorating, gratifying man, and seldom have I felt so keenly like him the truth behind Emerson's words, 'Great strength makes us happy'.

MARCEL PROUST'S
TRAGIC LIFE COURSE

(1925)

H E IS BORN in the dying days of the war on 10th July 1871, in Paris, son of a distinguished physician, from a wealthy, very wealthy bourgeois family. But neither the art of the father nor the immense fortune of the mother is able to rescue his childhood: at the age of nine, little Marcel loses his robust health for ever. Returning from a walk in the Bois de Boulogne, he is attacked by an asthmatic convulsion, and these terrible seizures crush his chest for the remainder of his life, right up to his final breath. Beyond his ninth year almost everything has been forbidden: travel, carefree games, acts of agility, high spirits, everything that is childhood. Thus he becomes an observer early on, sensitive, with heightened nerves, easily unsettled, a being with an acute irritability of the senses. He passionately loves the landscape, but rarely can he lay eyes on it, and never in spring: the fine dust of the pollen, the oppressiveness and gravidity of nature are too painful for his inflamed nerves. He loves flowers with a passion but he is not permitted to approach them. Even when a friend enters the room with a carnation in his buttonhole he is requested to remove it, and a visit to a salon where the table is adorned with bouquets forces him to retire to his bed for days on end. Sometimes he drives out in a closed car to see the cherished colours, the breathing calyxes from behind glass. And he takes books, books, books, to read about travel, of the landscapes he can never reach. Once he makes it to Venice, a handful of times the sea; but each of these trips costs him dearly in strength. So he finds himself virtually a prisoner in Paris.

His perception of all that is human becomes ever more delicate. The voice of a conversation, the clasp in a woman's hair, the way one sits at a table and stands up, all the finest ornaments of the social milieu affix to his memory with incomparable exactitude. The meticulous detail captures his ever-wakeful eye between blinks, all the connections, twists and turns, snaking around and pauses in a conversation remain lodged in his ears with their vibrations undisturbed. Thus, in his novel he can later keep up Count Norpois's conversation for one hundred and fifty pages and there is no pause for breath, no hesitation and no transition: his eye is alert and active on behalf of all the other exhausted organs.

Originally the parents decided that study and diplomacy would be the best course for him, but all intentions fail due to his ill health. But there is no immediate rush, his parents are well off, his mother adores him—so he squanders his years in society affairs and salons and until the age of thirty-five leads, in fact, the most absurd, foolish, futile, most aimless existence that has ever preceded a great artist, propelling himself as a snob through all the events of those wealthy idlers known as society, appearing everywhere and being received everywhere. For fifteen long years, night after night, he is to be found in every salon, even the most inaccessible, tender, reserved, always showing deference before the sophisticated set, always chatting politely, currying favour, amused or bored. Everywhere he is seen leaning in a corner, inveigling his way into a conversation and, strangely enough, the aristocracy of the Faubourg Saint-Germain tolerate the nameless interloper; and for him this represents the greatest triumph. Because outwardly the young Marcel Proust has no evident qualities. He is hardly good-looking or even elegant, he does not issue from the nobility and is to boot the son of a Jewess. Even his literary merit cuts no cloth, because his modest volume *The Pleasures and the Games* carries no weight and achieves no success, despite the backing of Anatole France. What makes him popular is solely his generosity: he drowns all the ladies with precious flowers, overwhelms everyone with surprise gifts, sends invites to all, pulls out all the stops to be complaisant and sympathetic even to the trivial elements of society. At the Hôtel Ritz he is known for his invitations and generous tips. He gives ten times more than American billionaires, and when he enters the hall all caps fly off heads submissively. His invitations are an excuse for fantastic extravagance and culinary sophistication, from all the stores of the city he gathers specialities—grapes from a shop on the left bank, spring chickens from the Carlton, fruit and vegetables specially shipped in from Nice. And he brings together *tout Paris* in an uninterrupted connection through courtesy and favours, without ever claiming a single one himself.

But what gladdens him even more than lavishly spending money within this society is his almost morbid reverence for its rites, his slavish idolatry of etiquette, the overwhelming importance he attaches to all the society people, all the nonsense around the fashionable set. Like a sacred text, he worships the unwritten *Cortegiano* of aristocratic custom; for days on end he might be consumed by the problems posed by a particular table arrangement, why Princess X had Count L placed at the bottom of the table and Baron R at the head. Every crumb of gossip, every fleeting scandal breaks on him like a world-shattering catastrophe; he asks fifteen different people to enquire about the hidden order of Princess M's invitations, or why that other aristocrat in her theatre box has received Mr F. And through this passion, through this seriousness applied to nothingness, which later also dominates his books, he gains the rank of master of ceremonies at the heart of this ridiculous and distraction-obsessed world. For fifteen years such a superior mind, one of the most powerful creators of our epoch, leads this inconsequential life among loafers and arrivistes, exhausted and febrile during the day, dashing between society events in the evenings, frittering away his time with invitations, letters and arrangements, the most superfluous man in this daily dance of the vanities: everywhere gladly seen, nowhere particularly noticed, in truth just a tailcoat and white tie in the midst of so many other tailcoats and white ties.

Only one element makes him stand out from those around him. Each night when he returns home and goes to bed, unable to sleep, he scribbles down notes upon notes, endless notes on all he observes, sees, hears. Suddenly they are whole batches of notes which he then groups in folders. And, just like Saint-Simon, seemingly a shallow courtier at the king's court, secretly he becomes the actor and judge of an entire epoch, every night Marcel Proust lists all the trivial and fugitive details of this *tout Paris* in notes and annotations and sketches, so that perhaps one day the ephemeral, the fleeting might be made permanent.

A question now for the psychologist: what is the primary cause here? Does Marcel Proust, a sick man poorly adapted to life, foolishly and vainly lead a snob's life for fifteen years for some inner pleasure, and are these notes purely incidental, a kind of after-indulgence of the all-too-soon-faded parlour game? Or does he enter the salons like a chemist the lab, like a botanist the meadow, inconspicuously gleaning material for the great one-off work? Is he faking it, or is he the real thing?

Is he just another combatant in the army of day's time-wasters, or a spy from some other higher domain? If he is a *flâneur* out of joy or pure calculation, is this almost absurd passion for the psychology of etiquette his whole life and need, or just the grandiose pretence of an impassioned analyst! Probably both found inspiration within him, magically conjoined as they were; for perhaps the pure nature of the artist would never have been able to express itself through him had not fate, with firm hand, snatched him from the airy game world of conversation and into the overcast, dark sphere of his own world, illuminated only from time to time by its inner light. For suddenly the scene changes. In 1903 his mother dies, and shortly thereafter the doctors determine the incurable state of his malady, which becomes ever more serious. With a sudden jolt, Marcel Proust pulls his life around. He remains cloistered like a hermit in his cell on the boulevard Haussmann, and from one day to the next the most bored *flâneur* and serial loafer transforms into the most embittered, dogged worker this literary century has marvelled at. Overnight he transforms himself from the most carefree sociability into the most draconian solitude. Tragic image of this great writer: always prostrate in bed, lying there the whole day, always complaining of cold, his thin body cough-ing, shaken by convulsions. In bed he wears three shirts, one on top of the other, ties cravats in a sort of wadding over his chest, on his hands thick gloves, yet still he is frozen, frozen. The hearth blazes, the window is never opened, because even the few wretched chestnut trees rooted in the asphalt wound him with their faint odour (which no other chest in Paris senses quite like his). Like a contorted corpse he lies in bed, always in bed, laboriously breathing the thick, over-congested, medicaments-poisoned air. It is not until late evening that he rallies himself to get up and see a little light, a little gloss, his beloved world of elegance, a handful of aristocratic faces. The servant helps him into his tails, enshrouds him in shawls and wraps his body, already three layers deep, in furs. So he sets off to the Ritz to converse with a few people, to revisit his deified sphere, luxury. Outside his door the driver waits, waits the whole night, and then takes the dead-tired man back to his bed. Marcel Proust no more attends society gatherings; only once does he do so, because he requires a certain detail concerning the precise bearing of a distinguished aristocrat. So he drags himself, to general astonishment, to a salon to observe the Duke of Sagan in order to discern just how he wears his monocle. And one night he visits a famous cocotte to ask her if she still has the hat she wore twenty years ago in the Bois de Boulogne, which he now needs to observe in order to furnish a proper description of Odette. He is downcast as she mocks him, saying she long ago made a gift of it to her maid.

From the Ritz they bring the exhausted man home. His nightgowns and cravats are draped over the ever-warm stove; he has for years now been unable to tolerate cold clothes. The servant wraps him up and leads him to bed. And there, holding the tray flat before him, he writes his wide-meshed novel *In Search of Lost Time.* Twenty dossiers are already filed along with drafts, the armchairs and tables before his bed and the bed itself are lavishly blanketed with slips and leaves of paper. And so he writes, writes day and night, every waking hour, fever in the blood, his gloved hands trembling from the cold, on, on, on. Sometimes a friend pays him a visit, he eagerly implores him for nuggets of society gossip, and, though fading away, he gropes with all his senses towards this lost world of sophistication. His friends become his hunting pack, informing him about this or that scandal, so he is kept up to the minute on this and that personality, and with nervous avarice he notes all they bring. And the fever becomes more intense. Increasingly, this poor, feverish being, Marcel Proust, decays and weakens, but the work on a grand scale, the novel, or rather the series of novels *In Search of Lost Time*, grows in strength.

The work was begun in 1905, and by 1912 he considers it complete. It runs to three volumes (but, thanks to expansion during printing, this swells to no fewer than ten). Now he is tormented by the question of publication. The forty-year-old Marcel Proust is completely unknown—no, worse than unknown, he has a poor reputation in the literary sense: Marcel Proust is that snob of the salons, the fashionable writer whose anecdotes about the salons appear from time to time in the newspaper *Le Figaro* (the reading public, scanning it quickly, inevitably mistake Marcel Proust for one Marcel Prévost). It doesn't bode well. There is little to hope for by taking the traditional route. So friends try another way, through social contacts. A well-positioned aristocrat invites André Gide, the head of the *Nouvelle Revue française*, the same which later will make hundreds of thousands of francs from the work, to view the manuscript. Gide rejects it out of hand, as does the *Mercure de France* and then Ollendorf. Finally, a new, courageous publisher emerges who is willing to take it on, but it still takes two more years to come to fruition in 1913, when the first volume of the monumental work sees the light of day. And just as success prepares to flex its wings, so war arrives and shatters them.

After the war, when five volumes have already appeared, France begins, Europe begins to sit up and take note of this most singular epic work of our time. And what glittering fame now surrounds the name of Marcel Proust, who for so long has been only a wasted, feverish, restless fragment of a man, a twitching shadow, a pitiful invalid, whose entire remaining strength is dedicated to seeing his work appear in print. He still drags himself to the Ritz in the evening. There, at the set table, or in the porter's lodge, he refines the corrections on the last printed sheets, for at home, in bed, he already senses the grave. Only here, when he sees his beloved sphere of sophistication shimmering before his eyes once more, does he feel a flaring of strength, while at home he collapses, broken-winged, soon fatigued by anaesthetics, sometimes reviving himself with caffeine for brief conversation with friends or to recommence work. His suffering only deepens and the pace of decline quickens, and he, for so long indolent, labours at a frantic pace in a desperate bid to outpace death. He no longer cares to see doctors, they have tortured him for too long and they never really made a difference. Thus he prepares to mount a final defence alone, and finally, on 18th November 1922, he dies. In the last days, already entirely given over to destruction, he makes a stand against the inevitable with the artist's only weapon to hand: observation. Heroically awake, he analyses his own state right up to the final hour, and these notes are intended to make the death of his hero Bergotte still more vivid, even more faithful to truth, to try and embellish the proofs with some intimate detail, details the writer cannot know, only one dying knows. His ultimate movement, then, is observation. And on the bedside table of the dead man, soiled by overturned medicines, one finds on barely legible notes the last words which he has already penned with half-cold hand. Notes for a new book that would have taken years, while only minutes were left to him. So he strikes death a blow across the face: the last magnificent gesture of the artist, who overcomes the fear of dying by listening in on it.

A THANK YOU TO
ROMAIN ROLLAND

(1926)

I HAD KNOWN HIM BEFORE. I had loved him before. Even then, in those carefree hours, I worshipped his work and was grateful, ashamed of his friendship as a gift not quite deserved. But I never experienced the full measure of the incomparable greatness of his spiritual presence until the darkest days of my life. Indelible, harrowing days in the abyss of war, I do not forget you, days when it felt like one must spew up one's own heart for shame and disgust, because, even faced with the disintegration of the world, one could be cowardly and low, desperately craving any excitation, no longer able to scream out from parched lungs—no, I will not forget you, you days of despair and shame of the soul, when everything was poised for the crash, had one thing not held fast the quivering spirit: the exemplary presence of this single European man. He was far away, inaccessible in those days of sealed borders; only a scattering of his words, his letters made it through, but, like a tiny speck of light buried deep in a mine, already confirming the existence of a higher domain, his clear-sightedness became a bright sky, his piercing gaze radiated over the mêlée with the deepening of innermost courage. And that tiny speck of light, that delicate star of hope shone upon countless such subsumed men, it provided comfort and uplift in numberless labyrinths, where each on his path, each led by his hand, gradually clawed himself upwards to the light. But to kindle such a sign of optimism required an inner amassing of fervour, of religious faith no other could muster in those days; in that moment we all became conscious of this man's human greatness, so long in the shadows.

And today, as always, again and again we see the wonderful magic of Romain Rolland, drawing the best out of people through the clear example of a pure yet impassioned life. He is the most dynamic being I have known; as a magnet draws iron from the slag, his presence, his wordless encouragement draws everything that sounds, everything that shines, all noble metallurgy from the chaos within our breast. What, according to legend, all books and times avouch as a miracle, that the man of pure will and indestructible faith says to him who has fallen beneath him, 'Get up and walk!'—this magic of the creative impulse he possesses in part in terms of a moral dimension. I do not believe that any artist of our day had such a purifying, strengthening and animating effect on as many people as Romain Rolland.

Each time I meet him I am both happy and ashamed. Each time I peer into his daily life, all seems incomprehensible in this crowding-together of a single existence. Above all there is the work, the relentless mental activity, which, like an inexhaustible well, alternately revolves its buckets, scooping up and then pouring out on the wheel of twenty waking hours. Then the mental curiosity, which encompasses five continents, all times and zones, which never falters and projects its clear, illumined gaze into what is most hidden. Then the friendship, tenderly attentive to every opportunity to gift the most appropriate joy in an unexpected moment, clear-sighted but also far-sighted, overlooking the shortcomings of those nearest. Then the unswerving righteousness, which is always tempered by goodness, this perennial awareness of all guilt, but without judgement or indignation. And above and in everything: passion, eternal passion for the sharing of each and every thing, in things and in people and in the invisible that hovers about us, in music. I cannot think of another human being worthy of my gratitude than this supreme human presence on earth, and I am overjoyed to find I am not alone in this stream of feeling.

A FAREWELL TO RILKE

Speech Given at the Munich Staatstheater

(1927)

MUSIC HAS SOUNDED at this hour, into music will it flow. Amidst its swaying melodiousness emerges the shy and bashful brow of the word. To this hour comes my own humble word, bowing deferentially to this precious and never-to-be-overgrown tomb. For only music is able properly to register the farewell we mournfully bid on this day to Rainer Maria Rilke, for only in him was the word perfected in music delivered to us all. Only on his lips was it redeemed from the mists of convention. Similes artfully raised the rigid body of language into the higher world of appearance in which every secret becomes palpable and our daily speech a barely comprehensible magic. All diversity knew how to shape it, his creative word, all forms of life sought their image in the sounding-mirror of his verses, and even death—even that emerged prodigious and objective out of the poetry as the purest and most vital of all realities.

But we, left behind in the lower element, know only the torpor of lament, lament for the poet, for him who, ever the divine one, seldom appears in our times and whom we were permitted to experience just once through the organs of the senses and the fervent strivings of the soul; with his form we have encountered something rare. For a true poet was Rainer Maria Rilke, absolutely he lives up to this ancient word—sacred, brazenly weighty and ambitious—which our dubious times all too easily confuse with the lesser and vaguer concept of the writer, the mere scribbler. A poet he was, Rainer Maria Rilke, a poet, over and again in the purest and most fully formed sense—as Hölderlin would have it, 'the divinely educated, impassive himself and light, but watched over by the ether and pious'. And so he was, not merely by the grace of the spirit but by the purity of noble life preserved within him. Poet he was and remained so, immutable and irrefutable in every word and in every act of his early life. Unlike many others, to whom the aura of such a proud name may be due, he was a poet not only in moments of exaltation, in those inconceivably rich intervals when the world plunges from the external to the internal; and in his astounded soul, ever the pure and restless artist, he always revealed himself, for truly there was no moment in his life when he was not a poet. Every word he spoke, every letter he wrote, every gesture that emanated from his delicate and melodious body, the smile about his mouth and the pure roundness of his writing, ever the same and unique, obeyed the same creative law as his verses their perfect shapes. In such a way, purity and unity radiated out to us, enclosed by crystals as transparent as his poem, and this unshakeable certainty of his mission drew us from an early age to defer to him, the man, the artist, and revere him. For, thanks to this omnipresence of beauty in nature and works, we have seen in him, in Rainer Maria Rilke, so unimaginable in our epoch, the unforgettable, authentic poet in face and in breath.

Poet he was always, Rainer Maria Rilke, and for all time. There was no creative beginning in his life when he did not deserve this illustrious name and the world did not perceive him as such. The pupil's childish hand hardly knew how to write, but already poems emerged. Scarcely had the down appeared on his lip than it spoke music. Relinquishing the play of childhood, he felt his way to a new kind of play, easy to start with and then becoming heavier and denser, a play with language, and to this boy it yielded, he who at all times would prevail. By the age of sixteen and seventeen he had already created verses revealing an accomplished melody, and long before his own physical being had been fully realized he had begun to achieve a distinct form in the creation of his spirit.

How this poetic genius began at such an early age, who can know? Who will dig deep enough into this mystery that stretches back into the darkness of our ancestors and the obscure origins of the earth? Was it the last stirring of the old blood, exhausted by succeeding generations, which, weakening, rolled in fully to enter the living, only able finally to fade away with a melodically rhythmic breath? Was it the shadows of the ancient lanes of Prague that lent a sense of the wonder-stricken to his youthful heart? Was it the Slavonic songs he heard in the fields at evening or those a maid sang, on Sunday, alone in the deserted room? Such traces are merely presumptuous guesswork, for who can possibly interpret the origin of a poet, this inconceivably strange being among people, in whom the thousand-year-old language newly re-emerges as if it had never been chattered to death on millions of lips, subsumed in millions of letters, until that moment when he appears, this One, who regards all things that have been and are yet to come with his astonished wonder, his rich palette, his rosy dawn gaze? No, this can never be explained by earthly causation, how, in the midst of a thousand dull beings only one becomes a poet, and why this one, in our midst and existing in the same orbit of time. A marvel enough always to dream up the unexpected, that the phenomenon of the poet occurs over and over to mankind and to think that this brother of our time was one of such a royal line, that in this slender, shy boy, constrained by the blue uniform of the cadet, beneath the awakening senses and in the midst of his blood there began to flow what later wonderfully broke over our feeling, where now it continues to murmur so impressively present that each of us, everyone has some line of verse or word of Rainer Maria Rilke's lodged unconsciously in their senses, a breath of music from him who no longer breathes and speaks and who will endure far longer than will our own insignificant existence.

This is how Rainer Maria Rilke had long since proved himself as a poet before that vocation properly laid its shadow across him, the seriousness and responsibility of the summoning word. They winged to his childhood, playful and light, the early verses, and he noted them down, just playthings between other games, in his carefully rounded writing. He wrote them out in schoolbooks and, still little more than a boy, carefully transcribed them in slender notebooks. And how wonderful, even that first note he struck found an echo among us, his peers, in a similar yearning and nervously wrought youth, and only now the consciousness of his mission opened his eyes and bade him look into himself soberly and demandingly. As a twenty-one-year-old he had already tasted fame, but he did not relish the sweetness and distractions of this dangerous mêlée, only the bitterness of responsibility did he draw from it and the sobriety of obligation. How early had this marvellous being grasped what the rest learnt too late or never at all, that the blessed gift which is granted the poet must be earned again and again through tremendous effort, so that he, by the most persistent and earnest application, is obliged to transform what genius initially gifted him as a game and on loan. And from that early realization Rainer Maria Rilke started out on that difficult road to perfection, of which he never tired and from which he never strayed—the highest honour bestowed for such pureness of dedication! Not even one step. It was precisely this quiet, mild-mannered man, this esoteric being, he whom the fools who preside over literary values had dismissed as a decadent, he who on the surface appeared tender, self-pitying and weak, who knew well the massive exertion necessary, as few of his contemporaries did, the effort which is the yoke of every creator if he wants to usher his own creative work into the world. He recognized at an early age, did Rainer Maria Rilke, that a soul had to fill itself interminably in order eventually to flow out of that fullness. He learnt early on that the poet, and he especially, must gather his senses and have them swarm like so many bees in order that the golden nectar of the poem would form in weighty, transparent and fluid shapes. Surely none of the lyric poets of his time considered the high price of perfection nor paid their dues more fully, as he who in his *The Notebooks of Malte Laurids Brigge* proposed the most sophisticated formula for the poem's design:

> Poems are not, as many think, feelings (you have them early enough). For the sake of a single poem, you must see many cities, people and things, you must understand animals, must feel how birds fly, and know the gesture of small flowers when they open in the morning. You must be able to think back on lanes in unknown places, to unexpected encounters, and to partings you had long seen coming; to days of childhood whose mystery is still unexplained, to parents whom you had to wound when they brought a joy and you didn't pick it up (it was a joy meant for somebody else—); to childhood illnesses that

began so strangely with so many profound and heavy transformations, to days in quiet, restrained rooms and to mornings by the sea, to the sea itself, to seas, to nights of travel that rushed along high overhead and flew with all the stars—and it is not enough even to think of all that. You must have memories of many nights of love, each one different from the others, memories of women screaming in labour, and of delicate, pale, sleeping girls who have just given birth and are closing. But you must also have been beside the dying, must have sat beside the dead in the room with the open window and the scattered sounds. And it is not enough to have memories, to forget them when they are many and to have tremendous patience to wait for them to come back. For it is not the memories themselves. Only when they become blood in us, gaze and gestures, nameless and indistinguishable from ourselves, only then can it happen that in a rare hour the first word of a poem rises up in their midst and goes forth from them.

With this sense of gathering in and listening for the sake of spiritual creation, the young Rilke moved into the world, travelling through all countries as the eternally homeless one, pilgrim of the highways. He was in Russia, so the bells of the Kremlin tolled in his poem, he has beheld the eyes of Tolstoy, searching the blueness through which thousands of images of people and destinies passed. He has seen Spain, Italy, Egypt and Africa, to experience all through a creative spirit and sense how the sun in those leafless lands makes altogether different paths of light than in our world of forests, he was in Scandinavia to witness white midnight nights, allowing him to perceive more deeply the blue dusk of southern valleys. He has been everywhere, almost always alone, rarely speaking, always listening, so that these fervent perceptions, all he absorbed in silence, will one day bear witness as words and music in the creative interaction of comparisons. No one knew where he was in those years of pilgrimage, the self-willed vagrant, and yet the work growing from within made it clear to all how deeply this observer had meanwhile penetrated the real and the changeable, for year on year his poems showed richer colours; and *The Book of Images* unexpectedly began that insatiable and inexhaustible richness of his lyrical speech, that great splendour of similes overflowing each other which no other lyric poet of our time has even come close to. The world which formerly the poet had merely registered as some vague presence in the sound of his emotions now drew closer, the senses became ever more alert, hearing and feeling, and thus he was able to write:

> Ever closer to me are objects
> And every form lies always before my gaze

But to regard them as isolated and detached soon became too modest an endeavour, for each simile, with its silvery-sounding chain link of rhymes, kept drawing in the sister of every phenomenon, a relentless certainty of one linked to the other, rounded out the loose scattering of all existence in space into a ceaseless stream, likewise into a fountain rising from the darkest depths of thought and at the same time illuminated by the highest lamp in the perpetual flow of renewed language. But the more powerfully this quiet creator grasped things, the deeper he drew them from the roots, the more he desired to give back in palpable form the comprehensible qualities of their evident forms, but also to interpret in a song-like fashion the inner power behind them, the cohesive and creative: the god. In numberless similes, with wings fluttering about him 'like clouds about the tower' in ever more urgent calls, in a sublime litany, his mystical ecstasy issues more and more appeals to this infinitude, and thanks to this visual artistic circling, from the still-isolated and fragmented forms of the *The Book of Images* finally arose that cathedral, *The Book of Hours*, that dome to God, perhaps the purest religious elevation that a poet has attempted in our times. The sea was found, the unfathomable, into whose infinite depths feeling could flow; from gentle humility came piety, 'the constant and silent gravity which works on souls from the depths of God'; from tender emotion came trembling, ecstatic intoxication; from individual stanzas moving musically on the wind came the bronze bell tolling of the great poem. To Angelus Silesius and Novalis, mystics turned towards God, he was a gentle brother and no less than they, risen as he was in the midst of a distinctly objective and factual German world.

This prodigious growth, over a few short years, from such a tentative beginning into a world-encompassing divine yearning for God, this self-advancement and sublime transformation our generation has witnessed in awe. It was marvellous for us to experience this, the rise of a poet in our time, and to be astonished anew year on year, ever more entranced, at how his unique art achieved fullness and fulfilment, as the first slender, miniature editions of his works blazed with images showing language permeated with colours; how the similes more and more consciously seized the kernel of every phenomenon, how from the fragile element of verse arose, sensually and effectively, the whole earthly world, and clearly pounding stanzas, with ever rarer and fresh rhymes, tethered the seemingly distant so fervently to that which is close by, truly as if our soul's existence was embraced by the most delicate membrane. And already we sensed that, beyond such creative verbal perfection, only a repetition of oneself, no real progress, was possible any more, for, just as trees with their fruit, these poems already bowed under the abundance of their rhymes, and the verses almost resounded with the overflow of music.

But before we dared to sense clearly that here a lyrical measure, a unique kind of finality in the poem, had been reached which no longer tolerated any excess and was only diminished by repetition, he, artist that he was, had already recognized the monumental danger. So there in the middle of the road, or rather at the height of his first perfection, Rainer Maria Rilke paused and began all over again, launched himself on a new lyric path, for even 'to rest in gravity', according to his own finely expressed term, was denied to this inadequate in excellence. That fate which one calls coincidence had at this hour directed him to Paris, where he had become the secretary of Rodin and resided in that vast, echoing hall in Meudon beyond the city, where the sculptures stood white and pure, a forest of stone, and yet each separate from the other through the emptiness of space and the inner finality of its contours. There he saw the master, the old man, with his dividing power, and he was tempted to follow his example and form his lyrical material as rigorously and concretely as that of the plastic, earthly effigies, to impose on the glassless, weightless element of verse a hardness of outline like that achieved in the heavy marble matter of earthbound stone. One realizes the courage of this radical redirection, for it is the complete opposite of what has until then been dominant. No more is Rilke concerned with the metaphysical connection and the metaphorical connectivity of things in earthly space, but rather undertakes to show the mystical conjoining of all appearance in the all-embracing feeling of the moment—an alarming prospect!—the fateful aloneness, the tragic detachment of each individual thing from the rest, and to realize it with cruel truthfulness. Thus, right in the midst of his vocation, he abruptly casts aside his own language as it had exhausted itself, in order to invent another, a new one; he steps boldly out of the vanquished element of music and into the still-unrestrained one of marble sculpture; the melodic artist in him recalibrates to assume a spartan hardness, above all he urges himself, his own being, his subjective compassion, to be drawn out of the poem, so as not to disturb with his own listening breath the sacred monologue that every being carries within them. For the poet, he senses, must not, in this new, more knowable phase, be the co-speaker in this new stone poem, not linguistically weave his statement with the compelling subject, but should in contrast remain silent and suppress himself in the work, so that the most authentic physical essence of each thing is complete. How beautifully does he formulate this stringent demand on himself and to all:

> O, ancient curse of the poets,
> Those who lament instead of speak
> Who judge their feeling instead of forming it
> Who still think what is sad in them or happy,
> They would know and should regret or praise it in
>   the poem.
> Like the sick they use a language full of plaint
> To describe the place where it hurts them,
> Rather than using stark words,
> As the stonemason of a cathedral doggedly
> Sets to work on the stone's equanimity.

Now, this is a new and heroically demanding task for the later Rilke: to transform himself, to dissolve completely into an alien form, no longer to bind himself sympathetically, and this 'form-alone' approach has left its work and wonder in the volumes of *New Poems*. On the marble bedrock of this book music is extinguished, snuffed out like a superfluous flame; now a factual light transparently delimits each appearance to an almost ruthless clarity. Each of these new poems stands and exists as an image wrought in marble, as a pure outline of itself, marked out on all sides and locked into its unalterable contours as the soul into its earthly body. These poems—I might just mention here 'The Panther' and 'The Carousel'—are cut out of the ponderous cold stone of their daylight like clear cameos transparent only to the spiritual gaze—structures that were unknown in German lyric poetry, the triumph of a knowing objectivity over the merely foreshadowing, something finite, a language that has achieved plasticity. Each thing stands there seamlessly and hermetically sealed in its own self, in its immutable heaviness. It no longer breathes music as in the past, only its indigenous form and the meaning of its soul are provided with an utterance of incomparable clarity which appears almost geometric. I say again, such poems were unknown in German poetry, in such unique and remote perfection, in such a sovereign reproduction of a sister art.

In this manner the tireless seeker had once again managed to bind the ambiguous world into a new, unanticipated order, and the poet would have gone on to shape thousands upon thousands of new formulas of these hundred lyric statues, every animal, every human, every single appearance of existence in its most original form. A ridge had been scaled in only a few years, the vertiginous lonely heights of perfection, and thus a cast was made which Rilke could easily employ for the whole world, form by form, till the end of his days; but again this creative seeker did not merely wish to be a reproducer of his own self, but knew himself to be 'the deeply defeated of the ever greater'. Once more, and for the third time, our withdrawn combatant heroically rejected his own creation, that which had ceased to be a challenge, to embark on a new lyric form and raise it to the unattainable infinite.

A decade ago, upon these majestic heights he began his last great poem series, the *Sonnets to Orpheus* and the *Duino Elegies*, rising to a self-imposed loneliness. For this outermost zone of the air of speech, this utterly alien antithesis of over-light and final darkness, was hardly likely to be followed by the senses of those familiar with lesser forms. So the Germans let him alone, and only a handful remained to discover what daring temptations constituted his visual mind in his last, most enigmatic poems. For here, in this sacred autumn of his final maturity, Rilke pushes language to the outer limits, trying to articulate what can scarcely be portrayed: not the sound vibrations that issue from things, not the sensual presence of form, but the mysterious connection that floats between them like a soul, as breath hovers above the lip. The wordless expressed through the word had failed, so his inadequate creative will sought to disclose a portrait of the merely conceptual, a metaphor of the no longer understandable. To achieve this, language had to be stretched beyond its own contours; it had to bow down to its deepest abyss, it had to go beyond the comprehensible and into the incomprehensible, that which was barely pronounceable. In the *Duino Elegies*, Rilke, who was once the lyric, then the Franciscan and finally the Orphic poet, is saturated with that sacred darkness which so magnificently flows over the verses of those other Germans taken from us prematurely, namely Novalis and Hölderlin. Scarcely could we at that time, over-whelmed, grasp the meaning which lay in those last poems, and only now does it open to our understanding: this was no longer the speech of the living, but a dialogue with the unknown beyond, the zone beyond things and feeling. It was already a dialogue with the infinite which rose here, a fraternal counter-speech with death, his own long-prepared and now-ripened death, which, demanding its due, raised its eye out of the darkness to meet that of the seeker.

This was his last ascent, and we can scarcely imagine the firn he conquered alone on this last venture. This spiritual con-summation felt like an ending, and he too sensed the need for rest. Language had offered him everything, he had exhausted its deepest enchanted source in his lyrical speech, imperiously imposed on it the most unutterable; so it was that, panting from the precipitous ascent, testing powers never quite exhausted, he now chose an as yet unmastered foreign language, seeking to find fresh rhythm in French stanzas, a new, even more demand-ing choice. Until the last moment a lover of the challenge, of the barely achievable, he selected this utmost effort purely as a means of rest, presumably with the intention that it would be an intermission before a new ascent to the infinite.

This tremendous heroic effort over twenty years, wholly dedicated to the lyric word, this tireless service of a poet to immortal, indelible forms, was only visible in Rainer Maria Rilke's work; the creation itself and his fate remained veiled. His inner life was a secret and no one saw him in his last workshop. His work grew in silence, emerging from apartness, as all perfected works must. This rare spirit knew that one had to be called, that the decisive creative work could only be accomplished through great renunciation, that the artist has to issue a determined refusal to the clamour of the day and renounce the immediate world, because, in his unforgettable words:

> For somewhere between life and the great work
> There stands an ancient enmity.

Powerfully life calls upon man, and all-powerfully it calls upon the artist, to remain objective and shape life into the visible; it wants a life attuned to the present, commands the poet to reflect its realities. Yet at the same time the poet is imperiously and jealously reminded of his still-unformed works, which are turned only to the future; where he is free from life, he refuses to answer life's demands and prefers to answer to the spirit, the artistic. All artists are faced with the decision of what attitude to take: commit to the permanent work or subscribe to the temporary animation of the present. Rainer Maria Rilke gave himself to art alone, the sacred other and the quiet asceticism of labour. The speakers' rostra barely knew his name, he remained alien to the stage and everyday work, his portrait was not in the marketplace, his voice was absent from every event and dispute of his time, thus few are those who knew his face, his life. Often he was in cities, in this city too, but something hidden went with him him which enveloped him, and no presence was as sentient as his, shy as it was and so filled with listening seclusion. Quietly he stepped into every room, whether in fear of disturbing or being disturbed you never knew, and even a conversation was more a display of genial listening than a stream of words. Often a kindly light smile played on his lips, but there was as much rejection and concealment in it as inviting love. One was fearful of getting close to him, so much deep silence seemed to insulate him, and yet how cheerful, clear, pure and fraternal was the word which issued from this silence and came to meet us. But never did he himself come forth, he who was demanding only in art and in life so modest. He was always the timid boy who sang, 'I am so fearful of the word of man.' Always fear hunted him, the violence of the real could surge too brutally against him and destroy the crystal-like vessel of silence that he carried around him. So he inclined into himself before the clamour and literature of our day, as though enveloped by a cloud. And like a cloud, silently and without pressure, reddened by the reflection of the infinite, he has passed.

As softly as he entered every room, as concealed as he was travelling through our vertiginous time, he has slipped away from us so quietly. He was mortally sick and nobody was even aware; even this mystery of his suffering, of his sickness, of his dying, even this he drew inside himself to mould into something poetic and beautiful in order to complete this last and long-prepared work in purity: to achieve his own death. It began quite early, this death in his narrow, secretive, life-worn body, the last and exhausted blood of his race, and it grew unstoppably and imperceptibly with his own growth. Sometimes this otherworldly voice spoke in the most mysterious of his verses, and then one heard that unsettling vibration in the midst of a poem, as with Keats or Novalis, the early departed, which never issues from the earthly. A ghostly sound, sweet and dark at once, sometimes flooded his words and verses, the ripple off a black bow in motion from other spheres, a speech, you might say, of wandering souls, for:

> Only he who has eaten poppies
> With the dead

Will never again lose
The softest tone.

The prose elegy of *Malte Laurids Brigge* on alien death, the dark verses of the *Requiem*, what were they if not anticipatory funeral dirges and clarion calls for his own death? He sensed it within, for years already, but, as with all feeling, he raised it to a great height and transformed it into poetry until it became mournful grief, and the premonition of mortality is itself immortality. We, however, listening rapt, were infatuated with this music, we loved the death growing in him unsuspectingly alongside his life and relished the rare sweetness, this blessed self-release, as a gift to us. And only when death roughly struck the world like a door suddenly slammed did we leap up and now regard the broken emptiness, the sheer poverty of our loss. But to contest this death, to call it premature and cruel, no, that he would not have wanted. We should stand before his death in awe, in reverence. As much as his death has deprived us of unsaid things, unspeakable possibilities, we must still be thankful to him for the lofty image preserved for us at the final hour, and that the memory of Rainer Maria Rilke stands as a perfected one before our love, an illustrious example to every young person that one can still be a poet, even today, in a world which has turned its back on poetry. He was this poet and remained so to the last breath. And the only consolation in our grief is that we may say: we did know him.

In the face of such a lofty, rare event even grief becomes humility and lamentation is flooded with gratitude. So it is not our wish to lament, but rather to offer praise to him from the depths of our grief; and as we cast the soil three times over the open grave, so let that of the word be dropped three times also. We wish to thank him in the name of our past, in the name of our present and the time that still remains to us. We wish to thank him:

Glory and reverence, Rainer Maria Rilke, for the sake of the past, which saw you grow through humility and patience from narrow beginnings to the greatest realization of perfection—an example to every youth and a model for every future artist!

Glory and reverence, Rainer Maria Rilke, for the sake of our present, you the rarest and most necessary, you once again showed the portrait of the poet as unity and purity.

And glory and reverence to you, Rainer Maria Rilke, pious stonemason at the eternally incomplete cathedral of language, for the sake of your love for the unattainable—glory and reverence to you for all the verses and works for as long as this German language endures!

NOTES ON
JOYCE'S ULYSSES

(1928)

I NSTRUCTIONS FOR USE: first you'll need a solid support so
you don't constantly have to hold this mammoth novel whilst
reading it, for this tome runs to almost one and a half thousand
pages and weighs like lead on your joints. Before settling in,
carefully select between second and third fingers the enclosed
leaflets declaiming 'The Greatest Prose Work of the Century'
and 'The Homer of our Time', then tear this shrill, overblown
promotional bumf to shreds and toss it in the wastebasket, so as
not to be irritated in advance by any fantastic expectations or
contradictions. Then install yourself in an armchair (because
it's going to take a very long time) and summon patience and
judgement (for you will be irritated too) then commence.

Genre: a novel? No, not at all: more a witches' Sabbath
of the spirit, a sprawling capriccio, a phenomenal Walpurgis
Night. A film of psychic situations, whirling and shrieking at the
speed of an express train, a stupefaction, a vast soul-scape brimming with the ingenious and the brilliant, a double-thinking,
a tripled feeling, a superimposition, confusion and quivering
of all emotions, a veritable orgy of psychology endowed with
a neo-technical slow motion which reduces every movement
and impulse into their atoms. A tarantella of the unconscious, a
raging and rushing flight of ideas, whirling along helter-skelter,
drifting on to whatever it meets, the most subtle and banal, the
fantastic and Freudian theology and pornography and lyricism

and the crudeness of cab drivers—a complete chaos then, but not dully dreamt out of some drunken, Rimbaud-like brain over-intoxicated with alcohol and demonically darkened, but boldly and deliberately orchestrated by a razor-sharp intellect, ironic and cynical. You cry out in rapture, you rage with exasperation, you wilt exhausted then are lashed on again, and finally you succumb to a kind of vertigo, as if you had been riding a carousel for ten hours or had listened to music unceasingly, the shrillness of the flute, then again that pounding, the jazz-band wildness, but always with intention is the modernist word-music of James Joyce, who here indulges in one of the most refined linguistic orgies ever undertaken in any language. There is something heroic about this book but also something that lyrically parodies art, that is justifiably a witches' Sabbath, a black mass, in which the devil apes and mimics the Holy Spirit in the most outrageous and ebullient manner, but one which is incomparable, unrepeatable, wholly new.

Origin: something evil at the root. Somewhere within James Joyce lies a hatred of youth, a primary effect of mental wounding. In Dublin, his home city, he must have profoundly suffered at the hands of those he hates, of the priests he hates, the teachers he hates, of anyone, for everything that this brilliant man writes represents a revenge on Dublin: his earlier book, the marvellously restrained autobiography of Stephen Dedalus, and now this horrifying psychological *Oresteia*. Not ten pages of geniality, devotion, goodness are to be found among the fifteen hundred, all are cynical, mocking, a hurricane of outrage, all explosive, inflamed by nerves already inflamed, all running at a heightened tempo which is both intoxicating and stupefying. Here a character not only discharges himself in a shriek, not only in the mockery of a grimace, but fairly vomits up his resentments, ejecting his emotional waste with a force and vehemence that causes the reader to shudder. The most ingenious bluff in detail cannot mask the tremendous sensation of emotion in this quivering, this vibrating, this foaming and almost epileptic temperament, by which a man here disgorges his book into the world.

Face: on occasion, in the pauses, I recalled the face of James Joyce; it suits his work. The face of a fanatic with a tragic eye, in ironic flight behind the spectacles of a myopic. A deeply troubled man, but hard as iron, rigid and tough, a lapsed puritan with Quaker roots, one who could be burnt for his faith and who views his hatred and blasphemy to be as sacred as his lost ancestors did their faith in the Church. A man who has lived long in the shadows, always alone, closed in, misunderstood, always submerged beneath his own time, which made his flame burn all the brighter. Eleven years of Berlitz language-school teaching, this most gruesome treadmill of the mind, a quarter-century of exile and deprivation have lent this art its sharpness and cutting qualities. There is greatness in his face and greatness in his work, a fantastic incommensurate heroism of devotion to the spirit, devotion to the Word; yet the true genius of James Joyce resides in hate and is redeemed only by irony, in one shimmering, wounding, anguished dagger-point dance of the mind, in a voluptuous violence of grief, horribly exposed and agonizing, a Torquemada lust of the psychological inquisition. The comparison with Homer leans more than the Tower of Pisa; yet there is something of the towering blocks of hate that is Dante in this fanatical Irishman.

Art: it does not reveal itself architecturally and pictorially, but only in the word. There James Joyce proves himself a veritable conjuror, a Mezzofanti of language; I believe he speaks ten or twelve foreign tongues and draws from them a completely new syntax and a rich vocabulary. He masters the whole keyboard, from the subtlest and most metaphysical expressions to the cackling of a drunken charwoman. He rattles down whole lexicon pages, sprays with machine-gun fire of attributes the terrain of every term, vaulting with stunning bravado the trapeze of sentence construction, and manages to pen a single line in the final chapter which I believe runs to over sixty pages (just as the entire tome only recounts a single day, the next book will supposedly recount the following night). In his orchestra the vocal and consonantal instruments of all languages are melded, all technical terms of all sciences, all jargon and dialects, here English, there a pan-European Esperanto. From up high to way below this gifted acrobat swings across in the flash of an eye, dances between clashing swords, leaps over all the abysses of the formless. The performance of the language alone attests to the genius of this human being: in the history of modern English prose, James Joyce inaugurates a unique chapter where he himself is the beginning and the end.

Summa: a moonstone, plunging headlong into our literature, a greatness, a fantastic, a sanctioned uniqueness, the heroic experiment of an arch-individualist, a maverick. Nothing of Homer, nothing whatsoever, whose art rests in the purity of line, whereas this flickering canvas of the spiritual underworld beguiles the soul just by its breathless rushing on and chasing-out of the past. No Dostoyevsky either, though admittedly closer to him in terms of the visionary imagination and that exquisite exuberance. Truth to tell, any comparison of this unique experiment ends in failure; the internal isolation of James Joyce will tolerate no attachment to anything; there can be no conjoining, and therefore presumably no descendants will emerge. A meteoric man, replete with dark, primordial power, a meteoric work of the Paracelsus type, like that medieval magician's writings in modern guise, weaving poetic elements with metaphysical humbug, spiritual mysticism with mystification, stupendous science with a grim jocularity. In short, a work more linguistically based than world-creative. But at least an immutable act: this book, an ingenious curiosity, will endure like an irregular block, detached from its productive-seeming environment. And if time is allowed properly to weather it, then it may become, like all that is sibylline, respectful of humanity. In any case, even today: respect for this idiosyncratic, emphatic and enticing performance, respect, respect for James Joyce!

ADDRESS
TO HONOUR
MAXIM GORKY

On the Poet's Sixtieth Birthday

(1928)

ALEXANDER PUSHKIN, the father of Russian literature, descended from royal blood; Leo Tolstoy from an ancient lineage; Turgenev came from the landed gentry; Dostoyevsky was the son of an official, but of noble line—aristocrats all. For literature, art, all forms of intellectual accomplishment were reserved for the aristocracy, like all other privileges, the countryside and palaces, rivers and mines, forests and fields, living human beings, peasants under the yoke who laboured under the sweat of their brow. All power, all wealth, all representation, all knowledge and evaluation were reserved for barely a hundred families of the nobility, ten thousand individuals in a land of millions. It was these alone who constituted Russia in the eyes of the world, her wealth, her race, her power and her spirit.

A hundred families, ten thousand individuals. But beneath this thin overlying crust slaved and laboured a boundless mass of millions, a sprawling, shapeless entity: the Russian people. Scattered in their millions over the interminable Muscovite plains, they toiled away, a million hands each day and each night, for the riches of the land. They felled the forests, levelled the roads, pressed the wine and drew ore from the mines. They sowed and reaped on the black or snow-weighted earth, they fought the czar's wars and, like other European peoples at that time, they unquestioningly served their princes in devoted labour and dogged serfdom. Yet one thing set this Russian people apart from their brethren: it was still mute, it had no means of speech. Long ago the other peoples had despatched spokesmen from their midst, orators and scholars, speaking tongues. These millions, however, still lacked the capacity to express their desires in written language; they were unable to make their thoughts heard in the councils of their lands; they could not explain themselves, could not articulate that great wild soul so alive within them. Dull, voiceless despite their straining breast, impotent with colossal strength, this ocean-wide mysterious being of the masses toiled and laboured upon the Russian earth, a spirit without speech, a being without conscious spirit. It was only the aristocrats, the powerful, who spoke for the silent. Until the twentieth century what we knew of the Russian people was articulated through the voices of their aristo-writers: Pushkin, Tolstoy, Turgenev and Dostoyevsky.

However, this fact will always be to the glory and honour of these aristocrats, who have never felt contemptuous towards the Russian people, the country folk and labourer, the 'lowly man', despite their dumbness, the silence imposed on them; but rather, as if from a sense of mystical guilt, each has shown an ardent devotion to the greatness and spiritual force of the lower orders. Dostoyevsky, the visionary, raised the concept of the people to a Russian saviour, to the symbol of an ever-returning Christ; bitterly opposing the bourgeois revolutionaries and anarchist noblemen, he bowed devotedly before the lowliest convict as representative of a divine power. Still more passionately did Tolstoy, the other aristocrat, show humble respect before the silent masses, abasing himself in order to raise the oppressed. 'The way we live is false, the way they live is the right one.' He cast aside his nobleman's robes and adopted the *mujiks*' smock; he attempted to imitate their simple, picturesque speech, their stolid, religious humility, to immerse himself, dissolve himself in this vast, life-affirming force. All the great Russian writers have with one voice expressed their awe in the presence of the great mass of the people, they have all felt something of the defencelessness, the speechlessness of their million upon million brethren, shadowing their own illuminated lives like a tremendous soul-guilt. They have all seen the great significance of their mission in the act of speaking for this unsophisticated, voiceless being and communicating its thoughts and ideas to the world.

But suddenly the miracle occurs, the unexpected, the unhoped for: suddenly this being, speechless for a thousand years, itself speaks. It forms lips from its own flesh, a spokesman from its own voice, sends a man from its midst, and this one man, this poet—its poet and witness—is thrust suddenly from the sprawling body so that he may convey greetings from the Russian people, the Russian proletariat, the lowly, the aggrieved and oppressed. This man, this human being, this messenger, this poet is suddenly present, emerging into the world sixty years ago, and with unfailing fidelity has for thirty years been the spokesman and painter of an entire tragic generation of the disinherited and downtrodden. To his parents he is Maxim Peshkov, but he calls himself Gorky, 'the bitter', and with this self-made name he is greeted today by the intellectual world and all those who feel themselves to be of the people within a people, for his bitterness has become a means of healing for an entire race, his voice an expression for a whole nation and his emergence a joy and a blessing to our spirit in this hour. Fate has plucked this one human being, Maxim Gorky, from the dregs and chaff of humanity to make him witness for the life of the oppressed, a painter of the misery endured by the poor of Russia and of the whole world. And to ensure he would be a faithful witness, it granted him every occupation, every ordeal, every privation, every test for his own being, so that his body might experience every affliction before he articulated them in poetic form. It despatched him to every proletarian province of labour, so that he might honestly present each to the invisible parliament of humanity. For long years it made him apprentice and servant to suffering before he could dare to become master of the word and of the form.

It was his fate to pass through all the changes and transformations of this proletarian destiny before he triumphantly morphed into the all-transforming one: the artist. So beyond artistic greatness, the rich and powerful work of this poet has the unique property of not having been bestowed by life, but by struggle, harvested from a miserable existence, and the pure and glorious result seems to have been drawn with bitterness from a hostile reality.

What a life! What depths before this ascent! A grimy, grey suburban street in Nizhny Novgorod witnesses the birth of a great artist; poverty rocks his cradle; poverty expels him from school; poverty casts him into the tumult and into the world. The entire family occupies just two cellar rooms, and to bring in a little money, a pitiful handful of kopeks, the schoolboy must crawl about in sewers and rubbish heaps, collecting rags and bones amidst the foul stench, so his classmates shun him, unwilling to sit beside the dung-collector and sewer-crawler due to the offensive odour. Though hungry for knowledge, he is unable to complete primary education and instead is obliged, with his diminutive, childlike form, to become a helper in a shoe factory, then houseboy for a draughtsman, dishwasher on a Volga steamer, porter at the docks, night watchman in a fishery, a baker's boy, messenger, railway worker, country labourer, printer's assistant, an eternally hounded day labourer outside of the law, downtrodden, homeless, a vagrant on every highway, now in the Ukraine, now in the Don, now in Bessarabia, now in Tiflis and now in the Crimea. Nowhere can he pause, nowhere can he settle. Barely has he secured shelter under some decrepit roof when fate like an evil wind whips him on once more. Winter and summer, he sweeps the streets with burning soles, hungry, ragged, sick and always hunted by poverty. Over and again he changes his job, as if fate itself has engineered these constant shifts so that he will possess the knowledge and experience to bear witness to every element of the proletariat's existence, the Russian land in its magnitude, the Russian people in its boundless diversity and multiplicity. It was his lot also nobly to bear the fate of those in Russia who revolted against the injustice of the situation; to languish in prisons, to be under police surveillance, to be spied on, hounded, placed under suspicion, hunted down by the police like a vicious wolf. As well as the lash of spiritual bondage, distorted opinion, this poet of the Russian people had to endure every form of suffering of his class and kind. He has to bear all forms of injustice and despair, even the final and most horrific, the highest and most profound despair known to mankind, when life becomes intolerable and is ejected from him like a bitter sputum. He is not spared even this last abyss of desperation. In December 1887, Maxim Gorky uses his remaining money to buy a pitiful revolver and with suicidal intent sends a bullet into his breast. It remains lodged in his lung, still threatening his life forty years later, but fortunately he was saved for the monumental labour, which he has accomplished alone, of bearing witness for his people before the tribunal of humanity.

When exactly this vagabond, this proletarian day labourer, this street urchin, this down-and-out became a writer no scholar will ever pinpoint with accuracy. For Maxim Gorky was always a poet by dint of the alert vision and clarity of spirit his generously receptive nature possessed. But to express this poetic material he first had to learn the art of speech, writing and spelling, and how laborious this necessity proved! There was no one to help him, only his stubborn will and the unyielding, unshakeable primal force which drove him on. As baker's assistant and street-sweeper he gathered by night all that came into his hands in the shape of books, newspapers, printed material. But his real teaching manual was the street itself, and his inner genius the real guide, for Gorky was a poet long before he had read a line and an artist before he had learnt to spell correctly. At twenty-four he published his first novel; at thirty he is suddenly discovered, already the artist most renowned and most loved by the people of Russia, the pride of the proletariat and a glory of the European world.

Indescribably significant was the impact of Gorky's early works, an upheaval, an alarm, a jolt, a rupture. Everyone sensed that a different Russia from that of the past was being written here for the first time, that this voice issued from the mighty breast of an entire people. Admittedly, Dostoyevsky, Tolstoy, Turgenev had expressed long before some notion of the Russian soul in its breadth and power. But now the same subject was treated in a different way, with more vitality and rigour; not only the soul, but the whole man is now laid bare, a naked Russian reality in all its gruesome clarity. With the earlier writers it hovered as a spiritual *ambiance*, in the tempestuous spheres of knowledge, the Russian soul, this limitless suffering, this extreme tension, the tragic knowledge of the course of world history—while in Gorky the Russian man rises not in the spirit but in flesh and bone; the shadowy, nameless person takes on definite form, assumes a cogent reality. Gorky, in contrast to Tolstoy, Dostoyevsky and Goncharov, has no comprehensive symbolical figures of world literature in the mould of the four Karamazovs, like Oblomov, Levin or Karateyev. Gorky's greatness is hardly diminished by the fact that he has never sought to establish a single symbol of the Russian, the Russian soul's inner nature, but instead has arrayed before us, so that we might grasp and touch them, ten thousand living forms of individual men and women with impressive perception and detail, with startling veracity and corporeality, for, born of the people, he has made visible an entire people. From all stages of wretchedness, from all levels of society, he has assembled figures, each unswervingly faithful to life, dozens, hundreds, thousands, a veritable army of the poverty-stricken and diseased; instead of a vision, one that is all-encompassing, this glorious eye returns to the living in a thousand individual forms each man whom he encountered in life. So this recollecting eye of Gorky is for me one of the true miracles of our world today, and I cannot see what in the art of our time can even vaguely rival in naturalness and exactitude his art of observation. No shadow of the mystic dims this eye; there is no blemish, no defect upon this marvellous crystalline lens which neither grows nor diminishes, which never interprets things wrongly positioned or askew; this eye never sees them too bright or too dark: only with clear and honest truthfulness. When Maxim Gorky draws the portrait of a man, I can solemnly swear: that is exactly how he was, no more no less; here nothing is added and nothing taken away, nothing embroidered and nothing deleted; here is captured the pure and unsullied uniqueness of a human being transposed into a portrait. There is no picture of Leo Tolstoy among his ten thousand photographs, not one account among the ten thousand penned by friends and visitors, which sheds light on his being with more discrimination, more vitality, more veraciously, than the concise sixty pages which Maxim Gorky has dedicated to his 'Recollections'. And, like this greatest of all Russians, whom he met, he has sketched with equal truth and justice the most wretched vagabond, the last gypsy he encountered as a hobo on the highway. The genius of Gorky's vision bears only one name: veracity.

To Maxim Gorky's incorruptible, marvellously honest vision, this truest image of the Russian world, Europe owes its gratitude; and when has there been a more urgent need for truth than at our present time, and what people have greater need of it than the Russian people in this world-historic moment? What an event, what providence, what a stroke of fate for this nation to possess in its defining hour a performer drawn from its own ranks, who reveals in black and white his own unembroidered image, one who is not sceptically mocking, who with a sense of the artist's committed justice draws closer to humanity as a whole, the yearning and hope, the peril and greatness of an immortal people. Tolstoy and Dostoyevsky, they have in their profound, penetrating and solicitous, confused nationalist passion created of the Russian people a devotional emblem, portraying the Russian man as something almost sacred, other-worldly, strangely powerful and dangerous, but always alien, of a different kind, with different judgements. But Gorky—and this is to his imperishable credit—depicts the Russian people not only as *Russian*, but crucially as *people*, interconnected with the poor and oppressed, the people as proletariat. He seems to belong more to mankind than to the purely national, he is more humanistic than political, a revolutionary through love of the people rather than bitter hatred. Unlike Dostoyevsky and Tolstoy, he did not see looming revolution as the product of a handful of impassioned anarchist intellectuals, as the practical realization of precise theories, but in his writings and his alone will future history ascertain that this revolt in Russia constituted an organic uprising of the people. He has shown how in the masses, through millions of individual details, the tension rose to intolerable levels: in his novel *The Mother*, his masterwork, the reader learns how from the humblest of men, from farmers, labourers, from the ignorant and illiterate, the will finds its tension in countless sacrifices without name, becoming ever more tense before finally rupturing and surging forth in a violent storm. Not the lone man but always the masses, always the multitude appear in his work as the arbiters of power; because he himself issued from the masses, from the fullness of the people, from the wide expanse of fate, this man perceives all happenings as communality. Even in this adherence to the people Gorky recognized, infinitely and unshakeably, the immortal power of his people. He put his trust in them as they did in him. While those great seers, Dostoyevsky and Tolstoy, trembled before the onset of the revolution as before a pestilence, he knew that the robust health of his country would see it come through. Because he understood the Russian people as a son his mother, from closeness or blood ties, Gorky never shared in the fearful apocalyptic shudder of anxiety common to Russia's great poet-prophets; he knew his people, and that all peoples possess the strength to lift themselves out of any crises, to survive all menaces. Thus his presence in the czarist years instilled more faith in the masses than all the piercing cries of Dostoyevsky for the Russian Christ, than all of Tolstoy's calls for repentance, his sermons of humility. The people took courage from his example and their confidence grew because of him. Maxim Gorky's relentless rise from the depths of the people has become a symbol for millions, and his work testifies to the determination of an entire people to lift itself and reconfigure itself in intellectual terms.

What we can affirm today is that Maxim Gorky has self-lessly offered himself for this service of testimony; a pure, honest man, an exemplary artist, never assuming a leadership role, never challenging authority as judge, nor arrogating to himself the trappings of prophet, but always a solidly reliable witness for the rights of his people, for its spiritual diversity and moral strength. A scrupulous witness, he has never denied nor played with the truth, never condemned but just reported. Without pessimism in the dark years and without exuberance in those that followed, robust in the hour of peril and shorn of pride in success, he has brought to life man after man in his work until they became a multitude, a people and an image of a people, the raw material of all form and creative power. Thus, his monumental epic is no hazy myth of the Russian soul, but unremittingly true, reality itself. It is due to his works that we can view Russia with a fraternal bond, a nation close to us, a neighbour to our world, without a sense of the alien, without antagonism; and here we see the highest obligation of the poet fulfilled, to eliminate all foreignness between men, to draw what is distant near, to unite people with people, class with class, until finally mankind is as one. Whoever knows Gorky's work knows the Russian people of today and through him the need and privation of all the oppressed; he knows with an understanding spirit its rarest and impassioned feelings as much as its penurious day-to-day existence. In Gorky's books we can tremblingly experience as in no others all the misery and trials of the period of transformation. Since we have learnt properly to feel with the Russian people in its most tragic hours, so today we can share in its pride and experience, share its joy as our own, the proud joy of a people, righteous and authentic, out of whose one blood came such a clear-sighted, plain-spoken artist. This spiritual festival of the Russian people is one for the whole world. So in this radiant hour, we greet two who are but one: Maxim Gorky, the poet created from the people, and the Russian people, who have become poets through him.

HUGO VON HOFMANNSTHAL

*Speech Given at the Commemorative Ceremony Organized
by the Vienna Burgtheater in Honour of the Poet*

(1929)

THE IMMEASURABLE LOSS which we suffered at the passing of Hugo von Hofmannsthal was, in those first few tragic seconds, more eloquently and passionately expressed than through words by our pain, our terrible shock, our restless distraction. Pain is always the most knowledgeable fortune-teller of every loss—with a single, surging blow it opens up depths of feeling, no longer illuminated by the following thought, and still less by the gradually remembered word. In this union of mortal wounding we were all intuitively aware, all Austria, all Germany, that something irretrievable had been stolen from us—but only now do we realize why that exemplary, pre-eminent figure has never been so irreplaceable as in the present hour. For a strange spirit, or un-spirit, now prevails in the time that wants only the temporal from art, always only the flowing image of its own restlessness and turbulence. Indifferent and hostile, our age passes by the great symbolic forms that remain immortal in the higher sanctum of the world. It has expelled the poem from its affections, and verse from the stage; it rejects the past and sacred convention, con-cerned as it is only with the present, the burning now, at best only with a glimpse of tomorrow. But this great man, Hugo von Hofmannsthal, stood alone against the current of the hour. Connected to illustrious ancestors, persisting in forms which he knew to be eternal, believing in those mysteriously

interpreted poetic signs which we term symbols, he stood solitary and imposing upon the German soil of classical tradition,
and it was only his higher bearing that kept the restless surge
of others in abeyance. He assumed this lonely vigil when that
other guardian of the exalted word, that other adored master
of the poem, the other great Austrian, Rainer Maria Rilke,
departed us. And this almost simultaneous, star-like vanishing
struck us as a warning, as if our belief in the higher laws of
art actually wished also to take leave of us at this moment, as
if the supremacy of pure poetry had passed, a sea change in
German literature.

But let us not forget our own higher meaning and fall prey
to confusion. There will and must always be a time when
nothing and nobody wishes to hear or see anything more
than their own realities, an epoch which prematurely seeks
to renounce the tradition of inherited laws, which believes it
can wrest itself from an eternal bondage to norms and forms.
Such a time has come often to Germany, and it was at just such
a moment that Hugo von Hofmannsthal emerged poetically
before the world. This precise moment was forty years ago.
The prophetic head of Friedrich Nietzsche was enshrouded
in darkness, the last German voice had fallen silent, the great
poetry created and the dithyrambic language ascended to new
glories. With this a new generation appeared, which immediately declared that language had no need of bondage to
historical roots or to be formulated with iron discipline to call
itself poetry. It could be plucked direct from the street, from
chance conversation, and something new and highly prized
was thus created and they named it Naturalism. It rejected
the pure, artfully formed architecture of the poem as a mere
plaything for an idle housewife; rudely it chased the classically

formed drama from the stage. Over time the classical works were lost to the archives and one by one interred. But then something happened which at first seemed insignificant. In a handful of minor journals in Brno and Vienna there appeared a scattering of poems and preludes, undersigned at first with strange pseudonyms: 'Theophil Morren', then 'Loris', and finally revealing the true identity of the writer as one Hugo von Hofmannsthal. A few poems, five or ten at most, found their way into these underground magazines. And, like an explosive force beneath the foundations, a little of their compressed energy sent out far-reaching vibrations, and in the briefest possible time these poems caused a palpable sense of excitement in the widest literary circles. But the nature and effect of a poem always remains an enigma. Millions of words surge through our world daily and fall back into the void, unredeemed, whirling dust. But on rare occasions, a few words, a few lines come together to create a living, breathing structure that miraculously outlives the lip which spoke them and those races who found pleasure in them. Such perfect poems, wrought by one man, showed themselves amidst this astonishing time. A new, enlightened voice appeared in the higher realm of German poetry and we were content to listen rapt to this new melody. Even as schoolboys we knew them, adored them, already idolized them, those morning-bright, beguilingly sweet verses of 'The Spring Wind', those dark verses looking downwards into their own sounding depths, the 'Tercets on Transience'. We knew by heart the Orphic stanzas of the 'Song of Life' and those landscape arias in *Death of Titian* in which the German language is at its most opulent and reveals a truly antique lightness of bearing. Everyone felt immediately that here was something perfect, unforgettable in the sphere of German literature, and in the possession of a nation which owes its vitality to this language. A whole nation was awestruck at the sudden revelation of this masterly talent. A poet had arrived, just at that moment when poetry of the classic style was regarded as impossible and outmoded, a poet who could encapsulate a universe of feelings with the most fragile and delicate material. Perfection always evokes awe, it always sends a peculiar, pious shiver through the heart. For wherever it reveals itself, in the immaculate beauty of a face, in the rhythm of a perfected body, in the quivering of a verse, in the melody of a song, always and everywhere humanity senses perfection as if the eye of the divine were resting on it here on earth.

However, even pious amazement in the face of perfection has its incremental stages; delight at perfection can yet grow. For the rational, clear-sighted mind can at all events find it comprehensible that on occasion a man, a proven and mature artist, achieves perfection as the result of and reward for count-less years of work. But it always appears as a true wonder, as divinely incomprehensible, when perfection is bestowed on a young man, one who is unaware, one instructed only by his genius.

At all times all peoples look to such young men as the only valid proof that the poetic will of the gods has become a reality on earth, that the supreme attainment can never derive from dynamically accomplished art but only with the gift of grace from on high. And even our own times, which long ago strayed from all things mythical, can today still call the magical appearance of the young Hofmannsthal a marvel. For now, forty years on, how can the rational mind make any sense of it, how to explain that this youth, a sixteen- or seventeen-year-old perched on a school bench filling his blue exercise book with Latin and maths, where still the teacher's red ink is visible, at the same time and with the same hand wrote on a separate sheet of paper some of the most immortal poems of the German language? How to explain that a boy's lip, yet to experience that of a woman, 'engaged in a lofty dialogue with the core and essence of all things', that at the same time as his graduation studies the adolescent created the eternal *Death of Titian* and soon after leaving school the *Death and the Fool*, the profound play that even today preserves its undiminished beauty?

And so wonderful, like the first beginnings, the years of tempestuously restless, splendid surpassing of the self over its own mastery. In this one decade, from his seventeenth to around his twenty-seventh year, one man did as much for lyrical writing as his whole gender, for alongside these first attempts—no, they were not just attempts, they were already accomplishments—came in blazing succession the profound plays *The Little Theatre of the World* and *The White Fan*, the lofty, echoing prologues, the colourful and substantial preludes, the first novella, so classic-Kleist in its prose, worthy of those poems by Goethe. And already the underground currents have begun flowing towards the dramatic works, to ever-more intense visions such as *The Marriage of Sobeide, The Adventurer and the Singer*, these works of opulence and extravagance.

No, never has a new poet, not perhaps since Goethe, created such an overabundance of visions, such an outrageous spiritual intoxication as Hugo von Hofmannsthal in his lyrical decade. Not since Novalis and Hölderlin has there been a lyrical poet bestowed with gifts from the gods, one blessed by music and anointed with the sacred oil of language; this man was right here in our city, in our country, and then his name burst forth into the whole realm of the German language and its time-transcending eternity.

The youth of Hugo von Hofmannsthal, was—let us not mince words!—a marvel, an incomparable, supernatural event. But the meaning of any true miracle lies in its uniqueness. Only seldom is such a miracle permitted to descend and dwell on this earth, and never for long, so that it does not wear itself out and degrade itself or lose its frisson and its heavenliness through repetition.

So it was impossible from the outset that this magical set of circumstances, this intoxication from work to work, could last for an entire life; for one so blessed, intoxication is blood bound to its element, youth. Inevitably a moment of change had to come because such a brimming-over with visions of the creative soul was no longer sustainable, and the lyrical drunkenness was obliged to give way to an orderly and conscious clarity. But this does not mean that the genius of the young Hofmannsthal had abandoned him completely, as with many others before him, Rimbaud, Lamartine, Uhland, whose poetic life was of short duration and who survived in an unfamiliar body. No, the entirety of the poetic power vested in Hugo von Hofmannsthal remained strong until the final moment, and furthermore it was illuminated and clarified by his ever-burgeoning spirituality; only that intoxication, that voluptuous excess of the first years ebbs with his passing youth, only that absent activity and that writing and formation, as it were, at the behest of transcendental powers. And nothing honours Hofmannsthal more than the fact that he never tried to recreate this magic state artificially and to artistically reproduce what had gone before. The intoxication is no longer in his soul, in his blood, and the determination to depart from this stage is interpreted so profoundly in that imperishable prose piece, the imaginary 'Lord Chandos Letter', where Hofmannsthal treats a similar phenomenon of mental switchover with wonderful psychological alertness. Never did a poet bid such a sincere farewell to the miracle of his younger self than did the mature Hugo von Hofmannsthal, obeying the higher laws.

A monumental, almost tragic commitment now faced the thirty-year-old. In an age which others timidly hailed, he had already achieved perfection in a poem, was unrivalled in prose, unsurpassable in those dreamy games of meaning. But now drama, the most powerful and demanding of art forms, threw down its gauntlet; now it was time for him to imprint on it the divine symbol of mastery. A truly superhuman aspiration drove him on, for Hofmannsthal was never content with average performances. How rigorously Hugo von Hofmannsthal addressed himself to this resolute aspiration, he who knew as no other the laws and values of a work of art; this moral achievement is obscured in his homeland by the deplorable reality that we here, in this enthusiastic city attuned only to lighter works, are obliged to witness stage performances only of those works in which the core of his creative will is not so persuasive: *Cristina's Homecoming* and *The Difficult Gentleman*, masterpieces of their genre, they are in the end just works wherein his spirit, delightfully modest, at the same time playfully and effortlessly relaxes its superior power and reposes in the light-hearted, the southern halcyon islands of his more northern creative world, which bestrides all times and zones. But to measure his entire oeuvre by them is about as unfair as constructing a four-tier symphony initiated by a line of scherzos. For Hofmannsthal's passionate will, from the very beginning striving even through pain, forged a Faustian dramatic world symbol in which all forces and counter-forces of existence conjoined. This dream, of one truly great global drama, a world theatre, preoccupied Hofmannsthal since his youth, for even *The Death of Titian*, which we are apt to view as little more than romantic playfulness, was only a sweet, melancholy foreplay to the tremendous symphony of life. The boy hero, who is coddled in a sphere of noble beauty, a higher-flown realm of art with as yet untainted hearts tuned to the rhythm of beauty, descends in the following scene into the city, immersing himself in the other world, the common one, so as to acquaint himself with daily life, dark and seedy passions; then the plague breaks out in this city and a torch of terrestrial passions is carried aloft aflame, the eighteen-year-old youth already dreams the drama on the vast scale of a fresco. *The Falun Mine* has remained a fragment and a second powerful drama in five acts, where likewise Faustian desire wants to rip apart the thin membrane between a person's body and the universe. Only in the summer of his life, perfected late but then wholly perfected, did Hofmannsthal create over seven years, in an incessant, incremental progression, his greatest drama: I speak of *The Tower*, that dramatic enigma which went far beyond the inadequacy of the stage, in which, inaccessible to most, a whole world of thought is embedded, this work with which he wrestled like Jacob with the angel and which left him, like Jacob, wounded.

An autumn perhaps, a golden ripening after this radiant and ever-inspiring beginning; after this powerful wrestling of manhood maybe this work would have matured into yet another; perhaps, as with Goethe, it would be the last age of wisdom, the dramatic aspirations of youth finally consummated. But between these last fulfilments and our passionate expectation the fate of his premature death intervened.

But while with unrelenting effort the artistic spirit seeks to wrest the drama's secret from it, at the same time the drama-turgically trained hand practises with strange, pre-formed styles. And we owe thanks to him for these recasting labours of immeasurable enrichment, a permanent prized possession for the stage. For, surveying the literature of all times with his far-ranging, humanistic, his truly magical, treasure-unearthing gaze, Hofmannsthal saw, where others remained oblivious, the golden ore within the rough rock, and he sought to increase his strength by reintroducing long-forgotten works of world literature to our own time, resurrecting and restoring them through theatre. How much, then, how infinitely much has this sacrificial service to the theatre come to our rescue! The *Elektra* of Euripides lay buried till then beneath philological rubble; only academics bothered to read it as a learnt text, it was deemed invalid for our theatre, our time. But he required only to raise this sunken treasure from the past and the Atreidean figure arose! From her royal gate in Mycenae she stepped into the midst of our time and made our hearts quiver with the momentousness of her destiny. Oedipus, Clytemnestra and Admet, eyeless statues of antiquity, as it were, who previously stood before us staring out larger than life, horrible and uncanny, through him received a new, more human regard, and in those mouths of stone something was now alive when he granted them language and the power of a soul out of his own. There was Otway's *Venice Preserved*, cast aside and virtually trampled on Shakespeare's path, a tattered, bloodied bastard of genius and linguistic inadequacy; but he bore it aloft, instilling it with the sultry breath that drifts over the Venetian canals and with the hot-blooded, tense and impassioned atmosphere of the Renaissance, and it morphed into a drama so powerful that some of its scenes seem to echo Shakespeare. Or his reworking of an old English religious play, *Everyman*, whose original author was forgotten. The people, the ordinary people came in their hundreds to the square before the church to audition for it and all literary portents were in accord that this was an extinct childish work, a mere game.

He took the forgotten relic in his adept, linguistic hand and instilled it with dramatic power using sublime woodcut verses, recalling those of Luther and Hans Sachs. And all of a sudden this *Everyman* appeared afresh to the world; every year thousands and thousands were summarily overwhelmed and deeply moved by it, one of the purest and most enduring dramatic constructs of our epoch. Just to stir it up, that is all this magician, this spell-breaker of the frozen needed to do and it suddenly came alive. Into *Dame Kobold* by Calderón he breathed new speech, and had her whirling across the boards with her adorable misunderstandings, charming every listener with her boisterous, roguish dances. All times and places, all shapes and spheres were a magical lure to his mind, from the orient and *A Thousand and One Nights* he brought the intoxication of starry nights into his *The Marriage of Sobeide*; from the magical world of ancient China mystery wandered ghost-like in *The Woman without a Shadow*. All this was not just about the wearing of masks and donning of foreign costumes, but real penetration of the subject; his language entered their rhythm, his soul their soul, like the commingling of blood.

Through this service to world drama Hofmannsthal brought incalculable profit to the German stage, not only in gloss, colour and passion, but more importantly because he encouraged our time to look back once more, to look back from the ephemera of daily dramatic output to undying mastery and that which is everlasting. But, as with his poetic brothers, he never shied away from commitment to the greatest achievement in language and music, and thus to imprint on the surviving form of opera the majestic form of poetry. We owe him our gratitude for the masterpieces *Elektra, Ariadne on Naxos* and *The Woman without a Shadow* issuing from the musical world of this time and all those still to come, and we owe him special thanks, as a nation, in our own city of Vienna. For Hofmannsthal, having apparently written only one libretto, created in *The Rosenkavalier* the most perfect Austrian comedy we have, our own Austrian *Minna von Barnhelm*, a truly national work magically reflecting colour and type, the upper class and those below, the nobility and the people, sweetness and cheerfulness, the whole brightly blended character of the city. Maybe people will say, narrowly: but a comedy merely for music, and only alive thanks to its presence! But can one imagine a bona-fide Austrian comedy without music? Take away the music from those works which hitherto have been hailed as masterpieces, Raimund's *Spendthrift* and *The Peasant as Millionaire*, the Hobel song, the Ashen song, the 'Little Brother', from Nestroy his jolly quodlibets, and you deactivate them, rob them of the finest, most delicate enamel. Music is always a vital part of an Austrian's soul, and for that very reason *The Rosenkavalier* is in its immortal fusion the defining symbol of our essence and being. So, in addition to the many aspects of Hofmannsthal's fame is the fact that, amidst his world-encompassing works, he has given his homeland the most enduring stage pieces of the time.

How many feats, how many works in one life, and yet that whole feat never the whole work! For what an elevated spirit, what a far-sighted thinker, beside the poet, have we lost in Hugo von Hofmannsthal—first revealed in his prose works. A winged spirit which rested only by floating and bridged every chasm, a spirit for which the upper element, which others only attain in short quick breaths, was its proper and natural home.

But this great spirit cannot be separated from his poetry, because they are formed, these incomparable writings, in that azure prose that only he can boast of, a prose that is so effortlessly, victoriously overpowering, to use his own expression, that it alternates with the universal language like the wind over a cornfield: prose which—and I say this with considered words—no one in Germany has written since Goethe.

Nowhere in German literature has more been said—let alone verse written—on the subject of the artistic, with more sovereignty and with such an eagle-perspective of the spirit, with such deep soundings of the world's conscience, as in these prose writings. The higher world which remains unapproachable to us all, there the true and self-evident sphere of his soul dwelt. That is why in the figure of Hugo von Hofmannsthal the art of our time has not only lost its most linguistic poet, but also its most clear-sighted judge, and there is no one in Germany today who can step into his shoes. Hugo von Hofmannsthal stands with the highest authority, distributing justice and order in a world adrift in the confusion of its own values, and at the same time he is the unwavering witness to the superiority of the mind over the spiritless, of purity and integrity shaping the chaotic and formless. Hugo von Hofmannsthal has demanded and demonstrated through his work that even today it is possible for a high one, a noble one, to serve the absolute in Art, and that we experienced this by his existence—therein lies the great commitment. For only when we let Hugo von Hofmannsthal's heroic passion penetrate the timeless and immaculate element within us as a vital power, only when we are accustomed again to exploring those lofty spheres where he creates and into which he has vanished—only then will we rightfully honour this now-departed and yet eternally present poet, only then will we be worthy to extol the memory of Hugo von Hofmannsthal.

ARTURO TOSCANINI

A Life Portrait

(1935)

'I love those who yearn for the impossible'

GOETHE

A NY ATTEMPT TO DETACH the figure of Arturo Toscanini from the ephemeral element of orchestral music and to fix him in the more durable substance of the word involuntarily draws us to the standard biography of a conductor. Toscanini's service to the genius of music and the almost magical power he exercises on every human community describe above all else a moral act.

For, in the figure of Toscanini, we have one of most veracious living artists in our contemporary world, who serves the immanent truth in the work of art with such fanatical fidelity, with such inexorable severity and humility, as we rarely observe today in any other sphere of the creative act. He serves art with pride, without arrogance, without self-will, the higher will of his beloved masters, and in all forms of earthly service: with the mediating power of the priest, the devotion of the believer, with the disciplined sternness of the teacher, the restless awe of an eternal learner.

Never is this guardian of the sacred archetypes in music concerned with a single element, only the greater whole; nor with outward success, but always with reinforcing the inner faithfulness of the work, and because always and everywhere he is not merely an individual genius, but one whose unique moral and spiritual energy performs exemplary deeds across the arts and for fellow artists. Here a tremendous personal triumph overshadows the musical space, becoming the supra-personal victory of creative will over the gravity of matter, marvellous confirmation that, even now in such fragile and fragmented times, a single being can create the miracle of perfection.

The realization of this immense task has seen over long years the necessary hardening of Toscanini's soul to an impressive and unprecedented restlessness. What counts for him in the arts is his moral greatness, chasing perfection is his human burden, nothing counts but the perfected work. Anything else, the somewhat praiseworthy, the almost perfect, the merely approximate, are not relevant to such artists, except in the sense of enmity. Toscanini despises conciliation in all its forms, he detests in life, as in art, tawdry self-satisfaction, complaisance, compromise. It is futile to remind him that perfection, the absolute, is in truth not attainable in our earthly sphere, that even the most grandiose will only gain an approximation of perfection, for it remains solely an attribute of God, strictly off-limits to the human; he will never, so wonderfully unwise, acknowledge this wise fact; for him there is nothing but the absolute in art. Like his demoniacal hero Balzac, he spends his entire life in this 'recherche de l'absolu'. However, every will that strains towards the unattainable, to make the impossible possible, achieves an irresistible power in art and life: only excess leads to the productive, never moderation.

If Toscanini wants it, then everyone else must too; if he commands, all obey him. It is unthinkable—as every musician in the shadow of his magic wand has testified—to be weary, casual or inaccurate, whether as co-creators or the appreciative audience; for under the spell of that elemental force erupting from him, through a mysterious transfusion something of his electrically concentrated energy flows into every nerve and muscle. Once turned to the work, Toscanini's will has the power of a holy terror, a force which first paralyses the overwhelming feeling, but then pushes it far beyond its own limits; with his relaxed tension he expands, as it were, the musical, emotional volume of every human being over the formerly accepted measure, he increases the power, the ability of every musician and, one might almost say, even of the lifeless instrument. From every score he brings out the most hidden and secret element; making his endless demands on each member of the orchestra, urging them to advance to the outer limits of their virtuosity, he forces on them a kind of fanaticism of work, an always higher tension of will and talent, which the individual, divorced from him, has never experienced so intensely and in all likelihood never will again.

One must realize that such violence of the will cannot be understood in a peaceful or leisurely fashion. Such an achievement necessarily presupposes a tenacious, savage, fanatical struggle for perfection. And it is a wonder of the world, one of the greatest revelations for every creative and reproductive artist, one of the few unforgettable hours of a lifetime, that one can visibly experience with Toscanini this struggle for perfection, this battle to get the maximum out of the maximum, thrilled, shaken, tense, observing all with breathless and startled admiration. In general, this struggle towards the perfect form takes place for poets, composers, painters and musicians in the confines of the locked workshop. From their sketches and manuscripts one may at most discern the sacred toil of the creative act. But at a Toscanini rehearsal one visually and acoustically experiences Jacob's wrestling with the angel of perfection, and it is always an imposing spectacle, terrifying and monumental as a thunderstorm. Whoever is concerned with art, in whichever sphere, will here receive an exemplary and incomparable encouragement of fidelity to the work when he sees with what violence, intensity and even brutality a single man driven by the demon of perfection draws music from every instrument, the highest level of skill from every player, with a sacred patience and sacred impatience forcing the merely approximate and blurred into the calibration of his own flawless, immaculate vision of the work. For with Toscanini—and this is his peculiarity—the conception of the work never arises again during the rehearsals. Every symphony of a master has long been elaborated inwardly, rhythmically and plastically to the slightest nuance before he even approaches the lectern; for him rehearsing no longer means creating but just bedding in and adapting this wonderfully precise inner vision, for Toscanini has already completed his sculptural work when the musicians are just embarking on their own. For weeks on end he spends long nights—this impressive body never requires more than three or four hours' sleep—drawing the score close to his myopic eye, working through it, bar by bar, note by note. His eminent sensitivity ensures every detail is perfectly balanced, his ethical conscientiousness applies itself to every emphasis, rhythmic nuance, in a way which verges on the philological. Now that the whole is complete in every permutation and inscribed on his incomparable memory, he has no further need of the score and can shed it like a cumbersome shell. For, as on a Rembrandt engraving, the faintest line, with its definite sharpness and depth, is bitten into the copper plate with that singular personal touch, so with Toscanini each bar is engraved on that most musical of minds when he mounts the rostrum. He knows with demonic clarity what he wants: now it is necessary to subjugate the others, will-less, to this will, his platonic model, to transform musical ideas into real vibrations of sound and impose as law on a multitude of musicians what he, the one, already hears within as spherical perfection. Monumental work, a seemingly impossible endeavour, an assemblage of the most disparate natures and talents must, with photographic and phonographic fidelity, feel and realize the ingenious vision of one man and in a unified way! But this one work, although magnificently performed a thousand times, is Toscanini's constant pleasure and torment: to bring into perpetual alignment a multiplicity of unifying forms; how, with heightened tension, he shapes what is indistinct to fullest clarity remains an unforgettable lesson for anyone who worships art in its highest form in terms of moral meaning. Only from these hours of struggle can one understand that Toscanini's work is not just artistic but also constitutes an ethical act. The public concerts show the expert, the artist, the virtuoso of his craft, the leader triumphant; they are, so to speak, already invasions into the subject realm of perfection. But only in the rehearsals is the battle for perfection properly waged; only in them is revealed the profound, the true, the tragic image of the struggling man; only in them does one see the courage and the rage of the swashbuckling warrior in Toscanini, his battlefields strewn with the turmoil of advances and setbacks, harried by the fever of success or failure in the work; and only here is mankind exposed through Toscanini's bared soul.

And in truth, Toscanini prepares to perform as if for battle; the moment he enters the concert hall he is outwardly transformed. If you see him at other times, alone or in an intimate circle of friends, paradoxically you might imagine this most sensitive of beings to be hard of hearing, since when he walks about and sits he gives off a distracted look, his arms are drawn in, his brow appears clouded, there is something absent in him, something remote from the external world. Unmistakable. Something is working in him, he listens, he dreams into himself, and all the senses are drawn inwards. If you approach him or speak to him he appears startled, the deep, dark eyes take half a minute or more to return from within and recognize a close friend; he is brooding, lost, hermetically sealed against all else but his inward music. A daydreamer, a work-dreamer, completely absorbed in the isolation and concentration of the creative and recreating artist. So Toscanini passes the hours. But at the moment when he raises the baton and faces the great task, this isolation is transformed into supreme connectedness, this languid, dreamy state gives way to the passionate will to act, he is now the commander, the dictator. Watchful, those otherwise velvety, dark eyes flash with fire beneath the bushy brows, around the mouth tightly stretch the creases of the will, on the hand every nerve is taut, all organs are in a state of supreme wakefulness, poised to attack as soon as he approaches the rostrum and with a Napoleonic regard measures his opponent—for the waiting mass of musicians seems at this moment nothing more than an ungovernable rabble which he must master, an involuntary, reticent entity on which one must impose strict discipline and law. He greets the gathering companions with encouragement, raises the baton, and in that very second— like a lightning rod with electrical energy sparking at its narrow tip—the will is hypnotically gathered in this magic stick. A single swing and the element is unleashed, his clear strokes rhythmically following the instruments. Now, further and further, you are already feeling, breathing with them. But a sudden stop, a rap hard and dry with the baton on the lectern, it wounds you, feels physical like a blow. The musicians pause in the midst of what to us seemed perfection. Then silence; a frightened void opens up around him and out of that silence now comes Toscanini's voice, weary, with an aggrieved, 'Ma no!' 'Ma no!', like a sigh of dejection is this 'no', this painful reproach. Something has awakened him, interrupted his vision, he is disappointed, the living sound that resonated audaciously with the instruments was not what Toscanini's inner ear wished to hear. Still, calmly, objectively, politely, Toscanini tries to will the musicians to understand his conception. Then he raises the baton, restarts at the delicate place, now the execution comes a little closer to his dreamt-of sound-image, but he has still not reached the ultimate point, still it will not correspond, the orchestral execution will not dovetail with the inner vision. Toscanini strikes again with his baton, more impassioned, more impatient, he demands clarity, more meaning. Gradually his powers of persuasion unfurl, the gestural skill of the Italian expresses itself magnificently in his body movements. Even the least gifted in music will already feel from his gestures what he actually wants and demands, when he beats the rhythm, when he imploringly throws out his arms then fiercely presses them to his heart again to demand the stronger accent, working his body in plastic terms to find the ideal sound image, visually modelling it so to speak. Ever passionate, he employs all his persuasive powers, he implores, conjures, begs, gesticulates, he counts, he sings, transforms himself into each instrument when he wants to emulate it, driving all visible movements on with wild gestures of his hands; a sculptor wishing symbolically to represent human desire and impatience, yearning, tension and fervent urgency would find no better model than Toscanini's tonal gestures. There can exist no more sublime model than these sound-image gestures of Toscanini. But if, despite these spurrings-on, this nervous agitation, the orchestra still does not grasp his individual vision, then the suffering of this earthly inadequacy causes Toscanini to fairly groan in agony. He groans like a wounded man, from his injured hearing, he works himself up till he is beside himself, for he is so utterly immersed in the work. He ignores all the inhibitions of civility because he sees only the inhibitions around the work, a fury against the dull resistance of matter drives him into uncontrolled language, he shrieks, he rages, scolds and insults, and you then understand why he only invites his friends to these samplings, where he knows he will always be dramatically vanquished in his monstrous, insatiable passion for perfection. The spectacle becomes still more shocking, this terrible wrestling match, Toscanini is ever more nervously excited, he physically attempts to wrest the dreamt form, the one he specifically heard, from the musicians. His entire body shakes with overheated nerves, like a fighter in the midst of battle, his voice becomes hoarse from incessant prompting, sweat runs down his brow, he seems worn out, old, after these immeasurable hours of immeasurable labour; but not even an inch away from completion does he relent until the dreamt-of perfection is realized. Instead he drives forward with renewed energy until finally the mass of musicians has absorbed his will and the vision is consummated. Only those who were able to observe this wrestling, this dayslong arduous struggle around rare and unique accomplishment, through its various stages can understand the heroic element in Toscanini and the price of achieving perfection, which the audience admires in him as a matter of course. The highest level of artistry is reached only here, where what is most difficult has the effect of what is most natural, when the most perfect has the effect of being self-evident. Toscanini in the crowded hall, magician and lord of the orchestra, effortlessly leading the hypnotized musicians—this triumph seems as if won without struggle and he himself appears the sum of all certainty, the highest expression of triumph. But in truth, no task is ever considered completed, no puzzle ever solved, for Toscanini, and what the audience finally admires and applauds as a definitive performance is already for him a problem. Despite fifty years of familiarity with these works, the seventy-year-old does not bask in full and pure contentment each and every time but savours the excited uncertainty of the new, the ever-seeking artist. Never does he experience a sense of easeful-ness, never for him what Nietzsche termed 'the brown fortune' of relaxation, self-enchantment. Maybe there is nobody among the living who is as affected by instrumental imperfection over the visionary as Toscanini, who has mastered the orchestra so magnificently. There are others of equable, passionate persua-sion among the conductors, but they at least enjoy fleeting moments of rapture. Bruno Walter, his Apollonian brother in musical terms, has, one feels, a few seconds of salvation and blessing in the midst of a performance. When he performs Mozart, one notices now and again how his face is uncon-sciously illuminated by a reflection of the light from this blessed genius. He feels himself borne on the self-created wave, he smiles without being aware of it, he dreams, he floats in the arms of the music. Such a blessing of forgetting is never granted to Toscanini, the insatiable one, the prisoner of perfection, and it is no artificial pose by this man of truth if, at the close of every concert, he retreats from the rostrum amidst the storm of cheers with an air of shame, a bashful and dismayed look, reluctantly and only for reasons of courtesy acknowledging the eruption of enthusiasm from the audience. For him, something hovers over all achievements, a mysterious, almost mystical mourning. He knows that even the heroic effort expended cannot find anchorage in the endlessly recreating element, thus he feels, like Keats, that his work might as well be 'writ in water', washed away in the waves of transience, disengaged from the senses, from the soul. In the end, no amount of success can beguile him, no triumph leave him intoxicated. He knows that nothing forged in the orchestral space is ever permanent, and every completion of a work must be recaptured and enforced hour by hour. How few are those who know this great absence of peacefulness. Art is an eternal war, never an end, always a relentless beginning.

Such a moral rigour of conception and character represents a significant event in the space of our art and life. But let us not lament the fact that such a pure and graceful appearance as Toscanini remains a rare one, and that only on a handful of days in the year is fortune granted to us and the perfected works of this consummate master are offered up to our ears. Nothing threatens the dignity and ethos of art more than the well-oiled and self-satisfied day-to-day art business, the ease with which radio and gramophone make the most exalted easy to consume at any hour; for this convenience leaves the struggle of creation forgotten, and art is merely consumed without tension or due reverence, like beer or bread. Benefaction and a certain spiritual voluptuousness should be seen at work in our time, and in the forcefulness of their appearance remind us that art is sacred toil, that such labour is an apostolic service to the unattainable divine of our world, not the gift of chance but earned grace, not tepid lust but also creative need. By virtue of his genius, by his indomitable nature, Toscanini has achieved the miracle of forcing millions to perceive the glorious, inherited heritage of music as the most vital artistic value of the present, and his act within the ensuing music fruitfully transcends its limits. What is gloriously accomplished in the space of art is made for everyone at the same moment. Only the extraordinary individual always leads the rest back to order and submission. And nothing leaves us more awestruck before this great advocate of faithfulness to the work than the fact that he has succeeded in instructing again even such a deeply troubled and incredulous time as ours to have reverence for its most sacred works and values.

MATER DOLOROSA

Letters from Nietzsche's Mother to Overbeck

(1937)

'This woman is truly inexhaustible in her patience—
and the patience that only a mother can boast is that which is required here.'

PETER GAST, 1890

A TIMID, SLIGHTLY BUILT pastor's widow in Naumberg, always she walks clothed in black, always she goes alone and most often to church, the pious, much-tested woman. Life has not dealt her a good hand. Early on she lost her husband, her daughter, her only one, the tender, cheerful Elizabeth abandoned her, emigrated to Paraguay with a strange dreamer, a forester; and the favourite son, the 'Fritz of her heart', alas, she sighs when she speaks his name and in church murmurs a special prayer for him. How much joy did he give her, the upstanding, clever, endearing boy. How proud she was of her Fritz in those early years: the most accomplished student in high school, the favourite of all the university teachers, at twenty-four a miracle in the academic world as professor at the University of Basel, honoured at the age of twenty-five by friendship with the famous Richard Wagner; every mother must have envied her for such a son, the quiet, modest, parochial widow in Naumberg. And what beautiful and learned books he writes, of course difficult to grasp for the naïve, traditionally minded old maid who has read little but pious tracts, at most the classics, and who misspells the titles of his works (*Twilight of the Mist* instead of *Idols* and *Zara Tustra* instead of *Zarathustra*), but all manner of learned people lavish praise on his writings, how can a mother not have trust in them? But suddenly her joy gives way to a wild fear, a sudden horror. First one appeared, then another, and declared that Fritz, her 'heartfelt Fritz', had dishonoured the memory of his devout father, writing scurrilously blasphemous books and sacrilegiously dubbing himself 'the Anti-Christ'. It was a disgrace, scandalous, a pastor's son had insulted the Christian doctrine and announced a crusade against the cross. The poor, simple woman is horror-struck to the depths of her soul; she has lost her living son and his letters seem so alien now, sometimes even severe. A wild, imperious tone flares up in his writings, in his being; a dark foreboding secretly creeps over the distraught mother, a demon, the enemy incarnate of God has taken possession of her child.

And suddenly the devastating news from Basel in January 1889, she must come, and now, right away. Overbeck, stalwart friend and, as professor of theology, the only one she has confidence in, brings the mentally sick man back from Turin, handing the madman over to his mother, to her alone, so that she can escort him to the living crypt, the lunatic asylum. Wretched scenes, which one is loath here to reproduce, take place at the reunion of the mother and deranged son she no longer recognizes. Anaesthetized by a powerful dose of chloral, accompanied by a doctor and an asylum warder, the sick Nietzsche is finally loaded with his mother into a coach and here begins his journey into eternal night; and also the story of the mother through her letters to Overbeck, one of the most overwhelming documents in the history of the human spirit (published under the title *Der kranke Nietzsche*, Bermann-Fischer Verlag, Vienna, 1937).

Terrible journey—outbursts of rage against the mother, so she is forced to move to another compartment—terrible the transfer to the madhouse, where for five marks a day the greatest genius of the century is confined in a cell. For the doctors, of course, he is not this genius, but an ordinary case of paranoia, with the note in parenthesis 'incurable'. The director of the institute, to whom they attempt to explain Nietzsche's true significance, at first refuses to read his works, saying: 'We have no time to waste on the writings of an aesthete.' A few days later they present to the students the case of Professor Nietzsche, a paradigm of paranoia, without anyone even recognizing the name 'Nietzsche' (which at that time was still so unknown that there was no entry for him in the encyclopedia). The patient is permitted to march up and down, and because his posture is not sufficiently erect, in order properly to display his symptoms, the professor pokes fun at him. 'An old soldier like you ought to know how to march with your chest out.' And the asylum warden ridicules the greatest spiritual man of our time, strokes his bushy moustache, claps him on the back and bear-hugs him, he who in his lucid life felt the slightest human touch as overly intimate and intrusive. Like Baudelaire's 'Albatross', who used to float freely and gloriously through the ether but whose wings are now severed, he has become an object of childish mockery, the target of the wardens' vulgar jokes. ('He crept many times into my head,' says his good-natured room-mate in a Saxon accent.)

'Incurable' and 'permanent internment', the doctors said. But there is one who does not care to believe it, the touchingly faithful one, the touchingly believing one, the touchingly tender woman, his mother. 'I am constantly tortured by the thought that the doctors may have pronounced the wrong diagnosis for my son's malady.' What are then these appalling foreign words, the findings? No, she does not believe it, because she does not want to believe that her child, the 'Fritz of her heart', is insane. It is merely that her adored son was overtaxed, and if she, the mother, were to take him into her care, he would recover his wits in no time. The doctors procrastinate at length. To leave a mentally ill individual with fearful outbursts of rage in her sole care (even Peter Gast worried that in this unhinged state Nietzsche might violently beat his mother or even kill her): well, it seems patently absurd. But the mother does not climb down, on the contrary she advances towards the danger, she bows before the cross she has imposed on herself and finally, early in 1891, the doctors agree that Nietzsche may leave the asylum, much calmer than when he entered it, but hardly recovered. From this day on his mother will become his sole carer.

And now sometimes you see this old woman leading the sick man like a great foolish bear through the streets and on long walks. In order to keep him occupied, she constantly recites poems which leave him stupefied; she skilfully steers him past the crowd, who gawp at him with curiosity, and past the horses which he dislikes. ('I don't embrace horses. I don't even like horses.') But she is happy whenever he is not causing a scene, when on the way home he conducts himself without 'loudness' (which is how she touchingly describes the demented yelling of the madman). At home he is easier to contain. If he is seated at the piano, the mentally absent one may linger there for hours lost in the void, and she is quite content with this, unless he plays Wagner, because she knows that Amfortas from *Parsifal* tends to aggravate his nerves. Or else she gives him something to read, which of course means that Nietzsche has no idea what he is reading, but simply to hold a journal or a book in his hands and mumble words from it tends to appease him. If one passes him a pencil, dark memories surge up in him that once he was a writer, and he scribbles and scribbles unintelligible words on the paper; something of the immortal poet, of the inner musician is still unconsciously awake in him, but as a ghostly presence, only the technical functioning remains. When he speaks he is usually confused and 'talkative', as the mother describes it; only now and then, as with the sick Hölderlin, shattering words flash through the clouds of nonsense. For example, when he states, 'I am dead because I am an idiot,' or, shaking the hairbrush violently, he cries, 'Comprehensively dead'.

All this the mother recounts to her friend in the most moving manner. She is sincere in her simple storytelling, yet one feels how the severely tested woman keeps silent about the more bitter aspects, how she always tries to paint Nietzsche's true state as brighter, potentially curable, and to her friend she hastily passes over his furious outbursts (when he exclaims, 'and with *what* a voice') in order to fabulate the notion of the 'good son', whose 'sweet face looks almost amused, even quite mischievous'. And it is only from those stifled sighs that one senses what an immense burden the mother has taken upon herself, to look after, to supervise, to wash, to feed, to clothe, to care for, to dress, all alone without the slightest outside help, to keep this up unceasingly for twelve hours a day and then, instead of resting while he sleeps, to take care of the household—one year, two years, five years, sacrificing her own life for the delusion of a recovery, without so much as an hour of freedom, without rest, without relaxation. 'Oh my dear,' she groans, 'none can imagine what I am going through.' Again and again she admonishes herself, 'So one must have patience and trust in the faithfulness of God's grace and all-powerful mercy.'

But finally this pious, miraculous heart can no longer be deceived, and relinquishes the long-cherished delusion that the 'Fritz of her heart' could awaken once more and regain his spirit. Resigned, she confesses that 'his suffering will always be a mystery to me'. She still keeps up the daily routine of service, feeding him ham sandwiches and caressing his cheeks. But more and more Nietzsche's powers are waning. He becomes ever more exhausted. He can no longer be lured out with the prospect of walks, but lies dumbly in his reclining chair, his empty eyes straining painfully towards any newcomer beneath heavy lids. The tantrums cease, the crater is all burnt out. Apathetically he sits or lies on the veranda. 'He has hardly managed a complete sentence in a month, physically he is collapsing, a sight to induce tears.' Eventually he feels nothing any more, no happiness and no misfortune; in a terrible way he is 'beyond everything'. The ability to distinguish between things begins to fail, the progress of dissolution is horrifying, even the concept of his own person is lost. 'He looks at his hands for a long time, as if they did not belong to him, then stuffs them in his trouser pockets, something he never did before. When this happens, I retrieve them, place them both side by side on the table, and if he nervously draws them back I caress them, carefully explaining that this one is his left and this one his right hand.' In vain now fame begins to seek him out, strangers make their pilgrimages to Naumberg, and the friends who misjudged him in his lucid lifetime now begin visiting—but it's all too late. He no longer recognizes any of them; like a dying lion, at once terrifying and magnificent, he peers out at friends and relatives, eyes failing. And fate spares the mother having to witness the final stage, the most terrible, as this living corpse, this immovable figure lies in the house until the moment when the heart ceases to beat in the semi-ossified body.

Shattering is this tragedy: a mind of the sharpest clarity, the most astounding wealth of knowledge, combined with the highest expression of language—and a tiny bacillus murderously devours this unique being, yesterday still beaming forth with creative strength, today destroyed, reduced to a state of animal dullness; an enigma, a mystery that not only this simple and gentle woman in her ignorance was unable to resolve and comprehend, but that we too look upon helplessly with unfathomable horror. There is something approaching a marvel, though, in the way she who remains oblivious to the incomprehensible, she the heroic mother, faithfully and selflessly continues the futile maintenance with undying strength, as she strives to force a miracle through humility and love; this heroism of love, no less powerful than the spiritual force of the great revolutionary, has now for the first time become irresistibly revealing in her letters to Overbeck. The unintentional gesture proves always the most beautiful and the most human. The purest emotions always issue from the simple, from the unadorned and factual truth and therefore we know more from these records of a simple woman than from all the clinical evidence and scholarly dissertations around the downfall and death of this mighty spirit of the past generation. The very one who perhaps understood him least in his work, the pious, the distant, the unsuspecting mother, managed through the miracle of love's power to come closest to delineating his being.

A FAREWELL TO
JOHN DRINKWATER

(1937)

L EAVE-TAKING is a difficult art, which the heart stubbornly refuses to learn; each time you stand with renewed trepidation before a fresh loss. Rarely, however, have I been shaken by the death of a comrade, a friend, and with such frightful suddenness as that of John Drinkwater. I really loved this English poet for his pure and humane verses and I greatly valued his dramatic works, of which only *Abraham Lincoln* achieved success at the Vienna Burgtheater. I admired him as Prospero and in other Shakespearean roles as one of the most sensitive and intelligent actors, and I was overjoyed at the friendship which bound us. I thanked him for the pleasurable times spent at his hospitable house, where one encountered the most distinguished artists of the time, and with the added presence of Daisy Kennedy, his wife, with her formidable talent as a violinist, the poetic atmosphere was made even more perfect. But one thing above all shook me on this occasion, and that was my final encounter with him just two days before his death.

It was on a Tuesday morning of the week before Easter when the telephone rang. It was John Drinkwater calling to invite me that afternoon to a private viewing for his intimate circle of a new film he had written for the coronation, *The King's People*. Naturally, I gladly accepted his invitation. The performance did not take place in a cinema, but in a small rehearsal room of the Warner Bros company, fifteen or twenty of us in all, installed in comfortable armchairs, with an atmosphere more akin to a chamber music recital. In addition to Drinkwater's closest relatives, there were the illustrious characters who starred in the film, Lady Astor and the eighty-one-year-old Bernard Shaw, fresh as ever—he had insisted on coming on foot from his apartment, marching all the way with those quick, stiff steps. A few more actors, the producer, then Drinkwater himself and his sweet eight-year-old daughter Penny, who boldly plays along in the film.

The opening scene of the coronation film takes place in John Drinkwater's house, because it deals with how the film came to be, a film within a film so to speak. Drinkwater appears as himself, explains to the American journalist the sense behind the coronation film, and while it rolls he consults with some eminent figures in England—Austen Chamberlain, Lady Astor, Bernard Shaw—who share their reminiscences from the period of Queen Victoria to the present. Now, there is something rather spooky about sitting in the same room with living people whose black-and-white shadows act and speak just two metres away on the screen. Just in front of me sat the eight-year-old child, Penny Drinkwater, gazing at herself embracing her father in the flowing images, who was actually stood, robust and alive, beside her. Bernard Shaw sat just behind me and smiled at himself—it was grotesque and uncanny at the same moment, this reflection of a double reality. Once, of course, that weird spell was lifted by candid laughter when the on-screen Shaw attends Drinkwater in the library room at the latter's house and—perhaps excusable for a man of eighty-one years—he happens to nod off. Drinkwater surprises him and is unsure whether to wake the patriarch at peace. Finally he does wake him, and right away Shaw fireworks Shavian paradoxes onto the screen, producing a wonderful comedic scene that no director other than that of reality could invent. As one we all impulsively applauded and turned around in that small room to the personable Bernard Shaw, who fairly sparkled with amusement between his tiny ears. A more relaxed and humorous mood could barely be imagined.

But then suddenly a depressed silence settled, like a ghostly bating of breath around the whole room. On the screen the maid appeared in Drinkwater's study and announced a new visitor—Sir Austen Chamberlain. Involuntarily all of us felt ill at ease. Austen Chamberlain had died just a few days earlier. Suddenly a dead man had entered our living circle. There he was, he fell back into an armchair (only the day before yesterday he was buried), lit a cigarette and began to speak. He spoke in a loud, clear voice, the dead man, he spoke with a carefree manner and with such clarity. All of us, I think, had a somewhat horror-struck feeling in our heads, we told one another: but you're dead, why are you living, why are you so impassioned, why are you talking? And we were all relieved when he departed the scene, and we rejoiced that instead of him, the living ones returned. John Drinkwater, full-set, bright of spirit, healthy, hugged his child and explained to her the significance of the coronation, the ideals of the Commonwealth founded on tolerance and entente. From Hades we had passed into the light and then there really was light in the little rehearsal room as the screen flickered out and the candles flared, the company shook hands sincerely with their friend, the author, John Drinkwater, one embraced the sweet little eight-year-old Penny, we respectfully helped the patriarch Bernard Shaw into his coat, then walked out onto the street and savoured the artificial light of the living night.

And on the evening of the following day, I said to myself: you must drop a line to Drinkwater and tell him honestly how nobly, with what decency, how poetically he solved the difficult problem of producing an official coronation film which could so easily have slipped into the byzantine, the over-patriotic, the tasteless. I also wished to thank him for having trust in me as one worthy to join that intimate circle of friends for whom this première was intended. I don't know why, but suddenly, urgently I had the overwhelming need to gift him a warm gesture, but for some reason I let it slip until the next day. So once more, and for the last time in my life, I received the admonition, never to hold back a gesture of friendship for a day, not even an hour. Because the very next day, in the street, from one of the hoardings, the words on the prominent announcement notice spelt out: 'John Drinkwater tragedy'. What tragedy? I wondered, alarmed. And so I learnt all for a penny: he had died that very night, and I had not even thanked him, not for this single occasion nor for the wealth of poetic attributes I have received from him over time. The one I saw yesterday, alive and buoyant beside the shadow play of his life, now he himself dwells with the shadows and our love gazes on him with distraught, confused and powerless hands that fumble in vain and sink down.

JOSEPH ROTH

Address to the Funeral Service

(1939)

T HESE LAST YEARS HAVE OFFERED MANY, indeed abundant opportunities to perfect the art of saying goodbye. How many farewells and how often to emigrants, outcasts, from the homeland, from our own sphere of activity, giving up house and property and all after the long years of hard-fought-for security. How many have we lost, always lost, friends through death or cowardice of the heart, and above all how much faith, faith in the peaceful and just configuration of the world, faith in the final and definitive victory of right over might. Too often have we been disappointed, still to hope in passion and ardour; and by some instinct of self-preservation we try to discipline our brain not to dwell too long on the next horror, swiftly to surmount each new shock and treat all that is behind us as ultimately dealt with. But sometimes our heart recoils at this discipline of rapid and radical forgetting. Whenever we lose a person, one of those rare ones, who we are aware is irreplaceable and irretrievable, we feel profoundly affected and yet almost buoyant knowing that somehow our downtrodden heart is still able to sense pain and to revolt against a fate which has prematurely robbed us of such an irreplaceable individual.

Such an irreplaceable individual was our dear Joseph Roth, unforgettable as a human being and an immortalized poet whom no decree could dislodge from the annals of German art. In him the most wide-ranging elements were assembled for the creative process. He came, as you well know, from a small town on the old Austro-Hungarian border; these origins had a determining effect on his spiritual formation. There was a Russian man in Joseph Roth, I would almost say the Karamazov type—a man of tremendous passions, a man who strove for the ultimate in everything. He was filled with a Russian fervour of feeling, a deep piety, but, fatefully, that Russian impulse for self-destruction too. And there was a second persona to Joseph Roth. The Jewish man with that bright, prodigiously alert, critical sagacity, a man of just and thus forbearing wisdom who was terrified to witness yet at the same time loved the wild, the Russian, the demonic nature within him. And yet a third element was at work in him: the Austrian man, noble and chivalrous in every gesture, as amiable and charming in day-to-day life as he was musically inspired in his art. Only this unique and impossible-to-replicate assemblage of elements explains to me the singular character of his essence, of his work.

He came from a small town, as I have said, and from a Jewish community on the borders of Austria. But mysteriously, in Austria the veritable confessors and defenders of the country were never to be found in Vienna, the German-speaking capital, but always only at the extremities of the empire, where men could daily draw comparisons between that easefully neglectful Hapsburg rule and the more severe and less humane equivalent in neighbouring lands. In the little town from which Joseph Roth emerged, the Jews gazed gratefully across to Vienna; there lived, as unreachable as God in the clouds, the old, the ancient Emperor Franz Joseph, and they venerated and loved this distant emperor like a legend. They honoured and admired the coloured angels of this god: the officers, the lancers and dragoons who brought a glow of colour into their tawdry, dull, wretched world. This reverence for the emperor and his army, a childhood myth, Roth carried with him when he travelled from his eastern homeland to Vienna.

He brought something else with him too, when, after untold hardships, he finally entered this hallowed city to study German at the university: a humble and yet ardent love for the German language, a love which is eternally renewed through his work. Ladies and gentlemen, this is not the hour to settle accounts with the lies and slander with which National Socialist propaganda presently seeks to throttle the world. But of all their lies there is perhaps none more pernicious, cruel and contemptuous of the truth than that which states that the Jews in Germany have demonstrated hate or hostility to German culture. On the contrary, it can be argued without any doubt that precisely in Austria, in all those borderland regions where the existence of the German language was under threat, the cultivation of German culture was sustained by Jews. The names of Goethe, Hölderlin, of Schiller and Schubert, Mozart and Bach, were no less sacred to these eastern Jews than to their patriarchs. It may have been an unfortunate love and certainly one poorly recompensed today, and whatever the lies of today's world, nothing can bury that love, for it is proclaimed in a thousand individual works and deeds. Even Joseph Roth's innermost yearning from childhood was to serve the German language and with it the great ideas that formerly spoke of Germany's honour, world citizenship and freedom of the spirit. This reverence had carried him to Vienna, his deep knowledge of the language which he quickly mastered. The slender, diminutive, reticent student attended the university where a comprehensive education was wrought from interminable restless nights of labour. But there was something else: his poverty. Roth was loath to speak in later life of those years of shameful deprivation. But we knew that until his twenty-first year he had never worn a suit tailored for him, only the shabby ones discarded by others, and that he had sat before his free meals, how often perhaps humiliated and wounded in his wonderful sensitivity. We knew that he could only continue his academic studies by frenzied bouts of teaching and tutoring. In the seminars he immediately caught the eye of the professors: a scholarship was swiftly awarded to this brightest and most accomplished student and he hoped for a lectureship. Everything seemed to be going his way. Then in 1914 the hard edge of the war intervened, which for our generation split the world into a clear before and after.

For Roth the war was both a moment of decision and liberation at the same time. Decision, because he had faced the prospect of a settled existence as a high-school professor or lecturer. Liberation, because it gave independence to him who was habitually dependent on others. The cadet's uniform was new and cut by a tailor. To shoulder responsibility at the front meant this modest, tender and timid man acquired for the first time a certain virility and strength.

But the fate of Joseph Roth was one of unending repetition, in the sense that whenever he achieved a position of security, it would be fractured in some way. The collapse of the Austrian army cast him back to Vienna, directionless, futile, destitute. Gone was the dream of university and gone the exciting episode of soldiering; now he had to construct a life out of nothing. He almost took on an editorship at that time, but fortunately Vienna seemed too slow-paced for him, so he decided to move to Berlin. There came the first breakthrough. At first, the newspapers merely printed him like anyone else, then they began to court him as one of the most brilliant, keen-sighted chroniclers of the human condition; to his good fortune, the *Frankfurter Zeitung* despatched him to far-flung corners of the world, to Russia, Italy, Hungary, Paris. It was then that we began to hear this new name of Joseph Roth for the first time. All of us sensed behind the dazzling technique of his depictions an overriding compassionate sensibility which delineated not only the appearance but also the life within, the innermost depths of man.

After three or four years our Joseph Roth possessed all that can be termed success in a middle-class existence. He enjoyed a partnership with a young and much-adored woman, he was appreciated and sought out by the newspapers, accompanied and welcomed by an ever-expanding readership, and he made money, even plenty of money. But success never made this wonderful man aloof, he never developed an obsession with money. Rather, he gave it away with both hands, perhaps because he knew in his heart that it would not be something permanent. He did not buy a house and had no home to speak of. Nomadically wandering from hotel to hotel, from city to city with his little suitcase, a dozen finely pointed pencils and thirty or forty sheets of paper, clad in his curious grey cloak, he lived the bohemian life of a student; some deeper knowledge disallowed every lodging, he suspiciously resisted every association with sedate and bourgeois contentment. And his own knowledge proved right, again and again, against every semblance of reason. Immediately, the first dam he had built against disaster, his young, happy marriage, was breached and gave way overnight. His beloved wife, this innermost anchorage, was suddenly struck down by mental illness, and though he wished to conceal the fact, it was incurable and permanent.

This was the first profound shock of his existence, and all the more catastrophic as the Russian man in him, that passionate Karamazov Russian of whom I spoke earlier, forcibly transformed this fatality into his own guilt.

But because at that very moment he tore deeply into his breast, for the first time he was able to liberate his heart, this wonderful poet's heart; to console himself, to bring healing, he sought to transform a meaningless personal destiny into an eternally renewing symbol; reflecting again and again on the question why fate struck him, and especially him, so hard, he who never harmed anyone, who in the years of deprivation had remained quiet and humble and who in the brief years of good fortune eschewed gestures of vanity, he remembered that man of his own race who turned against God with the same desperate question: Why? Why me? Why me?

You all know of course which symbol, which book of Joseph Roth I refer to, *Job*. This book, which has too hurriedly been labelled a novel, is so much more than mere novel or story, rather a pure, perfect poetry for our time, and, if I am not mistaken, the only work which has the capacity to outlast everything that we his contemporaries created and wrote. Irresistibly, in all countries, in all languages, the inner truthfulness of this representation of pain has been revealed, and this is our consolation amidst our collective mourning for the departed, that in this indestructible creative form a part of Joseph Roth's character is preserved for all time.

As I say, a part of the being of Joseph Roth is preserved in this work, protected from transience; and when I say part I mean to say the Jewish man in him, the man wrestling with the eternal question of God, the man who demands justice for our world and all future worlds. But now for the first time, conscious of his poetic power, Roth also undertook to bring forth the other man: the Austrian man. And again you know which work I am talking about, *The Radetzky March*. He sought to reveal through the figure of a last Austrian nobleman from an extinct race how the old aristocratic culture, which had decayed to its core, was ripe for destruction. It was a book of farewell, wistful and prophetic, as the books of true poets must be. Anyone seeking to decipher the inscription on the tomb of the old monarchy in years to come will do well to lean closer to the pages of this book and its sequel, *The Emperor's Tomb*.

With these two books, these two global successes, Joseph Roth had finally revealed the genuine poet within, the marvellously alert observer of that time and its mild-minded, benevolent judge. In those days fame and glory were heaped upon him: but they would never seduce or corrupt him. How clear-sighted he felt, and how indulgent at the same time, in every man, every work of art, recognizing mistakes, yet always forgiving, showing reverence towards the elders of his class, offering help to every young person. Friend of every friend, comrade of every comrade and well disposed even to the stranger, a real profligate of the heart, of his time, and, to borrow the term from our friend Ernst Weiss—always a 'poor profligate'. Money flowed through his fingers; when people lacked something, he instinctively helped them, for he was reminded of his former penury and the few souls who deigned to help him then. In all he said and wrote one sensed an irresistible and unforgettable kindness, the exuberant self-profligacy of the Russian. Only those who knew him in these times will understand why and how boundlessly we loved this one man.

Then came the turning point, the dreadful moment for us all, which had an even more profound impact on those more progressive, emotionally sensitive, world-embracing spirits who resolutely held to justice in the manner of Joseph Roth. Not so much that his own books were burnt and ostracized, that his name was brutally extinguished—not the personal dimension, no, what embittered and shocked him to the very core of his being was the doctrine of evil, the hate, the violence, the lie, that he was literally witnessing the Antichrist triumph on earth—it was this that propelled his life into a despair without end.

And so in this tender, gentle man, in whom affirmation, encouragement and kindness constituted the elementary functions of life, that transformation into bitterness and warlike struggle began. He saw only one more task ahead of him: to rally all his remaining forces, both artistic and personal, to combat the Antichrist on earth. He, who had always stood alone, who in his art had belonged to no group and no clique, now sought with all the passion of his wild and agitated heart to accommodate a fighting community. He found it, or thought to find it, in Catholicism and in the question of Austrian legitimacy. In his last years our Joseph Roth became ever more faithful, even a confessing Catholic, humbly fulfilling all the precepts of this religion, becoming a fighter and champion of the small and, as facts have proved, quite powerless group of Hapsburg loyalists and legitimists.

I know that many of his old friends and comrades have criticized him for this turn towards the reactionary, as they term it, and regarded it as an aberration and a product of confusion. But as little as I myself have been able to approve or even participate in such a term, I no longer pretend to doubt the honesty with which he approached it, and personally I see nothing unintelligible about his devotion. For he had long ago expressed his passion for the old, for imperial Austria in his

Radetzky March and had already shown in his *Job* that religious need, that will in the faith of God was the innermost element of his creative life. There is not a grain of cowardice, no agenda, no calculation in this transition, but only the desperate will to serve as a soldier in this struggle for European culture, whatever the rank or echelon. And it is my conviction that he knew with certainty, long before the fall of the second Austria, that he was serving a lost cause. But this was precisely what suited the knightly character of his nature, to position himself where it was both most innocent and most dangerous, a knight without fear or blame, utterly devoted to this holy struggle, the fight against the enemy of the free world, and indifferent to his own destiny.

He was indifferent to his own destiny and, even more, filled with a secret longing for a swift downfall. He suffered deeply, our dear lost friend, so inhumanly, so savagely in the face of the triumph of the evil principle that he so despised and abhorred, that when he saw the impossibility of destroying this evil on earth with his own powers, the urge to destroy himself took over. For the sake of truth, we must not gloss over it, not only Ernst Toller's demise was a suicidal act precipitated out of sheer loathing for our rabid, unjust and criminal time. Driven by the same overwhelming sense of morbid despair, our friend Joseph Roth also consciously annihilated himself, only in his case the period of self-destruction was much crueller, since it was dragged out, a self-destruction day by day, hour by hour, piece by piece, a kind of self-immolation.

I believe most of you already know what I seek to suggest: the tedium of despair over the unproductiveness and futility of his struggle, the inner disturbance caused by the turmoil of the world in recent years had left this alert and wonderful man a hopeless and ultimately incurable drinker. But do not imagine this word 'drinker' to mean the amiable imbiber who sits among a circle of comrades, sharing witticisms and gossiping, who entertains the group and instils in them a more vital sense of life. No, Joseph Roth's drinking was the drink of bitterness, an addiction to oblivion—it was the Russian man in him, the man of self-condemnation, who forcibly entered into bondage with these slow and sharp poisons. In former days alcohol served only as an artistic lubrication for him; occasionally he would sip cognac, but only lightly. At first it was just a means to an end, a trick of the artist. While others needed to stimulate brains which were not quick or visual enough, so he needed, with his tremendous clarity of mind, a gentle balm, calm nebulization, as when one lowers the light in a room, the better to appreciate the music.

But then, as the cataclysm overwhelmed him, there was a growing urge to blunt the inevitable, and the need to blot out his disgust for our brutalized world became a priority. For this he needed more and more of those golden and dark schnapps, always sharper and more bitter, to drown the inner bitterness. It was, believe me, a drink of hate and anger and powerlessness and outrage, an injurious, sinister, hostile drink that he himself hated but from which he was unable to wrest himself.

You might imagine how we, his friends, were shattered by this frenzied self-destruction of one of the noblest artists of our time. It is horrific to observe a loved one, a revered human being unable to defend themselves against all-pervading doom and ever-nearing death. But how awful only having to be a bystander to this destruction when it is not happening through uncontrollable outside forces, but is willed internally by the loved one. Unbearable to watch a friend's heart murder the rest of his being and not be able to haul him to safety. Oh, we watched him, this great artist, this benevolent man, externally as well as inwardly plunging into imprudence, clearly and ever more clearly the final fate was already etched in his dying features. It became an intractable decline, a slow destruction. But when I cite this terrible self-condemnation it is not to apportion blame, no, it is our time which is wholly guilty of our friend's downfall, this nefarious and lawless time, when the noblest are so desperate and despise the world so deeply that their only recourse is to destroy themselves.

It is not, ladies and gentlemen, in order to cast a shadow over the mental image of Joseph Roth that I have mentioned this weakness, but on the contrary, so that you might experience twice the wonder, even the miracle, of how magnificently indestructible to the last in this already lost man was the poet, the artist. Like asbestos before fire, the poetic substance in its essence defied the moral self-immolation. It was a miracle against all logic, against all medical laws, this triumph of the spirit created out of the already failing body. The very second Roth took up the pencil to write, all confusion ended, for immediately there was established in this undisciplined man an iron discipline practised only by the consummate artist, and Joseph Roth has left us no line which does not bear the seal of mastery. Read his last essays, read or listen to the pages of his final book, written less than a month before his death, and carefully examine this prose as one might a gemstone under a magnifying glass—you will find no flaw in this diamond's purity, no blemishes in its clarity. Every page, every line is like the verse of a poet hammered out with the most accurate awareness of rhythm and melody. Weakened in his poor, fragile body, agitated in his soul, he still remained focused in his art, with which he felt responsible not to this current world so hated by him, but to posterity: it was an unprecedented triumph over conscience, over the external decline. I would often run into him scribbling away at his beloved coffee-house table and knew that the manuscript had been sold in advance: he needed money, the publishers were pressing him. But pitilessly, the most severe and sagacious judge, he ripped the pages apart before my eyes and began all over again, just because some minor epithet did not seem to have the right weight, a sentence did not exude the fullest musical sound. Faithful to his genius as to himself, he has gloriously exalted himself in his art and risen out of his own death.

Ladies and gentlemen, there is so much more I would love to share with you about this unique man, whose continuing value to us, his friends, may not be fully understood at this hour. But it is not the time to indulge in definitive judgements now, nor to wallow in one's own grief. No, this is not the time for personal feelings, for we are in the midst of fighting a spiritual war, and I would suggest that we are defending the most exposed position. You well know that in war, with every defeat of an army they leave a small band of men to cover the retreat and allow the army falling back to reorganize. This handful of sacrificed battalions then have to withstand the pressure of the enemies' superiority for as long as possible. They are under the heaviest fire and suffer terrible casualties. Their task is not to win the campaign—they are too few in number for that—their task is only to gain time, time for the stronger columns behind them to regroup for the next battle proper. My friends, this forward defence position, this sacrificed post is now assigned to us, to us, the artists and writers of emigration. Even in this hour, we do not yet know what the inner meaning of our task is. Perhaps by holding this bastion we have nothing more to conceal from the world, than the fact that literature within Germany since the coming of Hitler has suffered the most miserable defeat in history and is about to vanish completely from the field of vision of Europe. But maybe—and let us hope so with our entire soul—maybe we only have to hold this bastion until the regrouping has taken place behind us, until the German people and its literature are free again and ready once more to serve the spirit as a creative unity. But be that as it may, we do not have to enquire as to the purpose of our task, for now each has but one thing to do: hold the post we have been assigned. We must not be discouraged when our ranks are thinned out, we must not yield and fall prey wistfully to our grief when the best of our comrades fall to left and right, because—as I said earlier—we are in the midst of a war and are holding the most dangerous post in the battle. When one of us falls, a glance across, a look of gratitude, sadness and faithful remembrance, and then back to hold the only hill that offers protection: our work, our mission, both our own and our collective work, to consummate them with upright bearing and virile strength to the bitter end, as did these two fallen comrades who show us by example the way ahead, our immortally exuberant Ernst Toller, our unsurpassed, unforgettable Joseph Roth.

WORDS SPOKEN
AT THE CASKET OF
SIGMUND FREUD

(1939)

IN THE PRESENCE OF THIS SPLENDID casket, permit me to say a few words of shocked gratitude in the name of his Viennese and Austrian friends, his friends around the world, in the language that Sigmund Freud has marvellously enriched and ennobled by his work. Above all, let it be remembered that we, who have come together here in mourning, are living through a historic moment which fate will never bestow on any of us a second time. Let us remember that in lesser mortals, in almost all of them, following the brief minute when the body cools, their existence, their being with us is ended for ever. On the other hand, with this one alongside whose bier we stand, with this one and only now in our desolate time, death means but a fleeting and almost substance-less phenomenon. Here, passing into the beyond is no end, no finite conclusion, but merely a lesser transition from mortality to immortality. For the physically ephemeral, which we are so painfully relinquishing today, the imperishable essence of his work, is saved by all in this room who still breathe and live, speak and listen, we are not as alive in spiritual terms as a thousandth part of this great man lying here in his mortal coffin.

Do not expect me to stand before you and praise the life's work of Sigmund Freud. You are well versed in that accomplishment, and who can remain unaware of it? Who of our generation could possibly deny that it shaped and transformed them inwardly? It lives on, this glorious discovery of the human soul, as an eternal legend in all languages and in the most literal sense, for where could a language exist that missed or lacked the concepts, the vocabulary, which he drew from the twilight realm of the unconscious? Customs, education, philosophy, poetry, psychology, all forms of intellectual and artistic creation and cerebral communication have been enriched and revalued by him over two or three generations as by no one else of our epoch—even those who do not know or even stand in opposition to his work, who resist his insights, even those who have never heard his name are unconsciously obligated to him and subject to his spiritual will. Each of us in the twentieth century would be entirely different without him, in their thinking and understanding, each of us feeling more constrained in our judgement, unfree, unjust, unable to think beyond ourselves, without that powerful internal impulse he left us. And wherever we attempt to penetrate into the labyrinth of the human heart, its spiritual light will continue to light our way. All that Sigmund Freud has created and foreshadowed as a seeker and guide will belong to us in the future; only one has departed us, the man himself, the precious and irreplaceable friend. I believe that all of us, no matter how different we may have been, craved nothing more in our youth as to see before us what Schopenhauer calls the highest form of existence—a moral existence: a heroic curriculum vitae. We all dreamt, as boys, of meeting such a spiritual hero on whom we could model ourselves and whom we could aspire to, a man indifferent to the temptations of fame and vanity, a man with a full and responsible soul purely devoted to his task, a task which in turn serves not itself but the whole of humanity. This impassioned dream of our boyhood, this even more severe postulate of our mature years, was filled by this dead man's life in an unforgettable way, granting us an unprecedented spiritual contentment. Here he stood in the midst of a vain and forgetful time, the unswerving one, the pure seeker of truth to whom nothing in this world mattered except the absolute, the eternally valid. Here he was at last before our gaze, before our reverential hearts, the noblest, the most perfect example of the explorer, with his perennial discord—on the one hand meticulous, carefully scrutinizing, seven times deliberating, self-doubting when he was not certain of a realization, but then, as soon as he fights to uphold a conviction, defending it resolutely against the entire world. His example has taught us, our age, once again in exemplary fashion that there is no more magnificent courage on earth than that of the free, the independent, the spiritual man; unforgettable for us will be his courage to find insights that others failed to discover because they did not dare to seek them or even speak or avow them. But he ventured and dared, again and again, against all resistance, ventured into the unknown until the final day of his life; what an example he has given us by his spiritual courage in the never-ending intellectual battle of humanity!

But we who knew him also knew what a touching personal modesty this courage possessed in the absolute and how he, this marvellous soul-strength, was at the same time the most understanding of mental frailties in others. This profound duality—the seriousness of mind, the goodness of the heart—at the close of his life yielded the most consummate harmony that can be attained within the spiritual world: a pure, clear, autumnal wisdom. Whosoever experienced him in these latter years would be comforted by an hour of intimate conversation on the absurdity and insanity of our world, and I often wished to myself in such hours that young people, the people to be, had also been present then so that, at a time when we can no longer bear witness to the spiritual greatness of this man, they might proudly state: I have seen a truly wise man; I knew Sigmund Freud.

This may be our sole consolation at this hour: he had completed his work and inwardly perfected himself. Master even over the original enemy of life, over physical pain through sureness of mind, through the tolerance of the soul, no less master in the fight against his own suffering as he was his whole life long against that of others, exemplary as physician, as philosopher, as a self-aware man until the last bitter moment. Thank you for providing such a role model, dear beloved friend, and thanks too for all your deeds and works, thanks for what you have been and what you have let permeate our souls—thanks for the worlds that you opened up to us, in which we must now walk alone without guidance, ever faithful to you, always remembering you with devotion, most precious friend, beloved master, Sigmund Freud.

DETAILS OF FIRST
PUBLICATION

The Return of Gustav Mahler
'Gustav Mahlers Wiederkehr', *Neue Freie Presse*, Vienna, 1915

Memories of Emile Verhaeren
'Erinnerungen an Emile Verhaeren', private printing, 1917

Arthur Schnitzler on His Sixtieth Birthday
'Arthur Schnitzler. Zum sechzigsten Geburtstag', *Neue Rundschau*,
Berlin, 1922

Frans Masereel: Man and Creator
'Frans Masereel. Der Mann und Bildner', *Neue Freie Presse*, Vienna,
1923

Marcel Proust's Tragic Life Course
'Marcel Prousts tragischer Lebenslauf', *Neue Freie Presse*, Vienna, 1925

A Thank You to Romain Rolland
'Dank an Romain Rolland', Eugen Rentsch Verlag, Erlenbach bei
Zürich, 1926

A Farewell to Rilke: Speech Given at the Munich Staatstheater
Abschied von Rilke, Rainer Wunderlich Verlag, Tübingen, 1927

Notes on Joyce's Ulysses
'Anmerkung zum Ulysses', *Die Neue Rundschau*, Berlin, 1928

Address to Honour Maxim Gorky on the Poet's Sixtieth Birthday
'Rede zu Ehren Maxim Gorkis—Zum sechzigsten Geburtstag des Dichters', *Neue Freie Presse*, Vienna, 1928

Hugo von Hofmannsthal: Speech Given at the Commemorative Ceremony Organized by the Vienna Burgtheater in Honour of the Poet
'Hugo von Hofmannsthal: Gedächtnisrede zur Trauerfeier im Wiener Burgtheater', Vienna, October 1929

Arturo Toscanini: A Life Portrait
Arturo Toscanini. Ein Bildnis, Herbert Reichner Verlag, Vienna, 1935

Mater Dolorosa: Letters from Nietzsche's Mother to Overbeck
'Mater Dolorosa: Die Briefe von Nietzsches Mutter an Overbeck', *Neues Wiener Tageblatt*, 1937

A Farewell to John Drinkwater
'Abschied von John Drinkwater', *National Zeitung*, Basel, 1937

Joseph Roth: Address to the Funeral Service
'Joseph Roth: Ansprache zur Trauerfeier', *Österreichische Post*, Paris, 1939

Words Spoken at the Casket of Sigmund Freud
'Worte am Sarge Sigmund Freuds Gesprochen, am 26 September 1939, London'

TRANSLATOR'S ACKNOWLEDGEMENTS

Above all, I should like to express my profound thanks to Linden Lawson, for her significant editorial contribution to these texts, the generous donation of her time to this project, no less her personal support and encouragement. In terms of the translation I should also like to acknowledge the invaluable assistance of Gesche Ipsen. I am grateful to Klemens Renoldner and the Stefan Zweig Centre in Salzburg for their help in providing certain elusive texts and to Dr Rik Hemmerijckx, curator of the Provinciaal Museum Emile Verhaeren in Sint-Amands, Belgium for assisting with my research surrounding the text 'Memories of Emile Verhaeren'.

WILL STONE is a writer, poet and literary translator of Franco-Belgian, French and German literature. His first poetry collection, *Glaciation* (Salt, 2007), won the International Glen Dimplex Award for poetry in 2008. Shearsman Books published his most recent collection, *The Sleepwalkers*, in 2016 and will publish a fourth collection, *The Slowing Ride*, in 2020. Will's translations include *Les Chimères* by Gérard de Nerval (Menard, 1999), *To the Silenced—Selected Poems of Georg Trakl* (Arc, 2005), *Emile Verhaeren: Poems* (Arc, 2013), *Georges Rodenbach: Poems* (Arc, 2017) and *Friedrich Hölderlin's Life, Poetry and Madness* by Wilhelm Waiblinger (Hesperus, 2018). His translations of Stefan Zweig with Pushkin Press include *Montaigne* (2015) and *Messages from a Lost World: Europe on the Brink* (2016). Pushkin has also published his translation of *The Art of the City: Rome, Florence, Venice* by Georg Simmel (2018) and *Surrender to Night: Collected Poems of Georg Trakl* (2019), as well as producing new editions of *Journeys* by Stefan Zweig (2019), *Rilke in Paris*, including 'Notes on the Melody of Things', by Maurice Betz / Rainer Maria Rilke (2019) and *On the End of the World* by Joseph Roth (2019). The complete cycle of *Poems to Night* by Rainer Maria Rilke will be published by Pushkin in 2020.

Will has contributed poems, translations, essays and reviews to a range of publications including the *TLS*, the *Spectator*, *Apollo Magazine*, the *RA Magazine*, *The London Magazine*, *The White Review*, *The Poetry Review* and *Modern Poetry in Translation*. His essay on the Belgian painter Léon Spilliaert as illustrator appeared in the catalogue to the exhibition 'Léon Spilliaert' at the RA, London, in February 2020, and was translated into French for the catalogue to the exhibition at the Musée d'Orsay, Paris in the autumn of 2020.

MORE FROM

STEFAN ZWEIG

The
World
of
Yesterday
Memoirs of a European

STEFAN
ZWEIG

PUSHKIN
PRESS

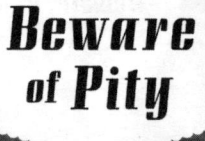

STEFAN ZWEIG

Beware
of Pity

PUSHKIN
PRESS

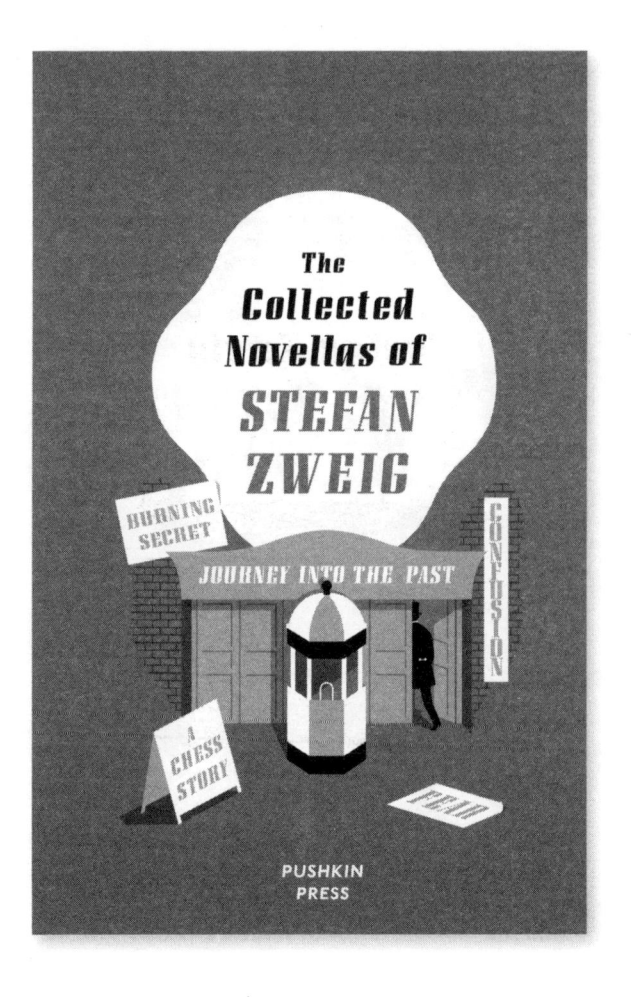

The
**Collected
Novellas of
STEFAN
ZWEIG**

BURNING
SECRET

CONFUSION

JOURNEY INTO THE PAST

A
CHESS
STORY

PUSHKIN
PRESS

'Zweig's
celebration of the
brotherhood of peoples
reminds us there is another way'
The Nation

Stefan Zweig
JOURNEYS

PUSHKIN
PRESS

'Stefan Zweig's
time of oblivion
is over for good...
it's good to have him back'
Salman Rushdie

Stefan Zweig
NIETZSCHE

**PUSHKIN
PRESS**